Con

ALERT! This book contains FYIs for NCPs. It is informative, resourceful and offers practical advice to aid non-custodial parents who provide support for their children. This book offers examples of real life NCPs who have overcome enormous obstacles in the process of paying child support and will teach you how to do the same! Read to find out why:

- a $56,000 arrearage of a so called "deadbeat" had to be dismissed by the child support agency
- the agency had to reduce the arrears of various NCPs
- the agency had to reimburse payments to NCPs in many cases

"Author, Marty Vaughn has shown why non-custodial parents must become familiar with child support enforcement practices, and has shared experiences to demonstrate the need and benefits of personal case monitoring and payment tracking. Organizations that provide assistance to non-custodial parents will also find this book to be an excellent source of information. Lawyers that work in this field will find this book to be a useful resource as well."

~L. E. Maioriello,
Attorney at Law
Martinez, GA

"Marty's book is a well-organized and informative resource for non-custodial parents with equally insightful, useful and beneficial information for custodial parents, lawyers and paralegals."

~L. D. Wiley, Attorney
Washington, D.C.

"Through <u>Child Support Dollars and $ense—Show Me the Money!</u>, author Marty Vaughn has compiled what is frustrating and overwhelming into this no-nonsense book. It reads like a reference book! Well done!"

~S. Kingdom, Executive Administrator
and custodial parent
Augusta, GA

"Using Marty's practical advice in <u>Child Support Dollars and $ense—Show Me the Money!</u> helped me resolve a problem in my case that went on for two years. I have been case monitoring and payment tracking ever since."

~T. Buie, Business Owner and
non-custodial parent
Baltimore, MD

"Marty Vaughn couldn't have created a more timely or useful resource than this one. I've never read a more accessible book on such a complicated topic."

M. Johnson, Director and
custodial parent
Tucson, AZ

"When you read a book, if the writer is able to not only teach you about the subject, but make it understandable, that writer has hit a home run! I believe that is what Vaughn has done with <u>Child Support Dollars and $ense—Show Me the Money!</u>"

~B. D. Williamson
Evans, GA

"I found Marty Vaughn's <u>Child Support Dollars and Sense—Show Me the Money!</u> both informative and interesting . . . wonderfully structured with case studies ranging from the ridiculous to the surreal, followed by wrap-up and recommendations from someone who has been in the trenches."

~T. Shaffer, Administrator
Oklahoma City, Oklahoma

"Marty Vaughn has what it takes to give non-custodial parents great advice: years of work assisting NCPs in understanding legal implications; a know-how and willingness to share information that is of benefit; and a dedication to work with and for parents who need help managing their role as a non-custodial parent."

~C. Isaac, Director
Augusta, GA

Child Support
Dollars
and
$ense

Revised Edition

—— Child Support ——
Dollars
and
$ense
Revised Edition

Show Me the Money!

A Practical Guide for Non-Custodial Parents

MARTY VAUGHN

authorHOUSE®

AuthorHouse™
1663 Liberty Drive
Bloomington, IN 47403
www.authorhouse.com
Phone: 1-800-839-8640

While I have labored at length to provide the most recent and accurate general information available, there may still be mistakes. Therefore, I make no guarantees as to whether or not information will still be current at the time you read this book. Please use this book as a general guide and not as a definitive source of information relating to your situation.

Published by AuthorHouse   03/25/2013

ISBN: 978-1-4817-1876-9 (sc)
ISBN: 978-1-4817-1875-2 (e)

Dedication

This book is dedicated to my children
and grandchildren.

Table of Contents

Introduction

This book is written out of my personal experiences with the child support enforcement agency personally and as an Intermediary Research Agent and Paralegal assisting non-custodial parents just like you.

People often ask how I got started or what the first case I ever investigated was. Oddly enough the first case I ever investigated was my own. I was a divorcee at the time with three children. I had previously received public assistance for about two-and-a-half years before I began receiving child support. My child support payments were by wage garnishment and things went well for about two years. Without warning, the support payments just stopped. My ex insisted that payments were being made, but the child support agency insisted that they were not. Choosing to believe the child support agency, I contacted my ex to give him the business (you know what I mean), but before I could do that he presented me with several recent check stubs that reflected that the payments were still coming out of his check. I contacted the agency with this information and was told that their system did not show any of the payments and that the employer likely made the deductions, but neglected to send them to the agency. That was quite a stretch seeing that my ex and the agency both worked for the same employer . . . the state government. In the meantime, my ex's tax refund was intercepted for alleged arrears. At this point I was fed up; I couldn't afford an attorney and refusing to sit on my hands, I launched my own child support case investigation.

It turned out that my ex had told me the truth about his payments and there was no employer oversight. However, there was an administrative error. The support payments for my case had been applied to the wrong accounts. This meant that other people were receiving my child support payments! Upon further investigation it was found that the amount of time that I had received public assistance had been overstated, and therefore the reimbursement debt to the state had been miscalculated. The agency adjusted my account and credited all the payments. Also my ex was refunded the tax refund that had been improperly intercepted. So, that is my story in a nutshell.

This book comes after many years of providing assistance and seeing a consistent need for every non-custodial parent to become more involved in the business of their child support case.

This book is designed to provide general information on the importance of personally monitoring your child support case, tracking the payments you make to that case, getting organized, staying organized, and more. I have also shared a few stories of cases I have assisted in throughout the years that you may find interesting, to say the least.

It is my hope that by using the strategies I have outlined, you too will be able to effectively manage your situation as it relates to your child support case. This book contains a lot of information from a variety of noted sources that I hope you will find useful.

CHAPTER 1

Show Me the Money!

Each year the child support enforcement administration collects billions of your dollars in child support payments. Unfortunately, millions of those dollars go undistributed for various reasons. In fiscal year 2010 more than $26.6 billion [1] in child support payments were collected. In that same year net undistributed collections (see Chapter 3) reached over $5.6 million[2] Of that net undistributed amount, over $381 million held the status of "pending distribution" while over $175 million remained unresolved and therefore undistributed.

Unresolved, in this situation, means that those funds could not be distributed to the intended parties—the children! Any unresolved collections that do not find their way to their intended parties can be escheated to the state after as little as 180 days time (in some states). This means that a clerical error in some office somewhere or your own negligence could result in the money you are paying not reaching your child and eventually becoming the property of the state, permanently.

We all understand that even the most principled and thoughtful human beings make mistakes. With all due respect to child support enforcement agencies, they are no exception to this rule. As long as caseworkers continue to deal with high-volume caseloads and system conversion errors, and until the integrity of agency audits and clerical and data entry errors are improved, administrative errors and oversights can and should be expected to occur. Even so, no system (especially a public system such as child support enforcement) should be allowed to benefit from its own errors or inefficiencies. This is fundamentally unfair.

So, if you are making child support payments you would do well to consider those payments as important as you would any deposits being made to your own bank account. After all, you have a vested interest in both.

While the system is imperfect, it is the only one we have. It is vitally important that NCPs pay child support and any advocate of an alternative to that would be horribly misguided in this author's opinion.

Sitting around raising your fists and forming organizations to point fingers will not change anything. Do your part to hold the system accountable for the child support payments you make.

The only way to make a difference is to become more involved with your child support case and to follow up on the payments you make to your case. There are things that you can do to ensure that the payments you make to your case reach your child. Let me stress the importance of continued civil communication between you—the NCP—and the CP if at all possible. With some notable exceptions, the only way for you to know definitively that the funds you contribute are making it to your child is through the CP.

This book is a timely and much-needed resource for NCPs who are seeking answers and assistance as they continue to provide support for their children. There are several case summaries noted throughout the book. Through them, you will get an opportunity to read about the experiences others have had regarding their child support cases. I always felt like a handful of the cases I had assisted with over the years were fit for Ripley's Believe it or Not! If their experiences do not convince you of the importance of consistent, thorough case monitoring and payment tracking—NOTHING WILL!

Also, if you think that the task of monitoring your own child support case is somehow not your job, think again.

REFERENCED IN THIS CHAPTER

[1] Child Support Enforcement FY 2005 Preliminary Report

[2] OCSE Preliminary Data Report Table P-32 Net Undistributed Collections (UDC) FY 2010 <http://www.acf.hhs.gov/programs/cse/pubs/2010/reports/preliminary_report_ fy2009/table_32.html>

CHAPTER 2

Paternity, Child Support and Visitation

Establishment of Paternity

Legally the matter of paternity is fundamental to the issuing of any child support order, and it is important for you as the NCP to understand exactly how the matter of paternity has been established in your case. Per federal statute, state procedures should require "the establishment of paternity of a child at any time before the child attains 18 years of age[1]."

There are several established and accepted practices used by the child support enforcement administration to establish paternity:

Voluntary Acknowledgment of Paternity—Generally, this procedure is conducted through paternity establishment services offered through "hospital and birth record agencies" by a "simple civil process" where acknowledgment is obtained by signed affidavit. A signed acknowledgement[2] is also a basis for seeking a child support order. And, because the acknowledgment is legally binding the window for challenge is very small. It "may be challenged in court only on the basis of fraud, duress, or material mistake of fact, with the burden of proof upon the challenger . . . [3]."

Be that as it may, this does not deter NCPs from seeking proof of their status as biological fathers, especially in areas where a decision of paternity is based on "non-genetic testing factors." In fact, there are many cases regarding this very issue being challenged all over the country.

The United States Code puts it this way:

> State[s] must provide that, before a mother and a putative father can sign an acknowledgment of paternity, the mother and the putative father must be given notice, orally, or through the use of video or audio equipment, and in writing, of the alternatives to, the legal consequences of, and the rights (including, if one parent is a minor, any rights afforded due to minority status) and responsibilities that arise from, signing the acknowledgment. [4]

The Uniform Parentage Act of 2002 allows minors to execute a Voluntary Acknowledgement of Paternity without the signature of a parent or guardian [5]. This is troubling, because a minor may not enter into any other sort of binding contract without parental consent. The relative lack of experience the average teen has relating to what any long term contract entails is a problem by itself. When you consider that this acknowledgement involves the life of a child and has potentially far reaching implications well into a minor's adult life, it is shocking that such an admission is allowed without the input of a responsible adult.

Genetic Testing[6]—The genetic testing method is a blood test in which deoxyribonucleic acid (more commonly referred to as *DNA)* is used to determine the paternity of a child. This test may be requested by either party, the administration, or the court ("in a contested case.") Some states may use this method as a requirement for paternity establishment. This procedure should "create a rebuttable or at the option of the state, conclusive presumption of paternity upon genetic testing results indicating a threshold probability that the alleged father is the father of the child[7]." The "threshold probability" is usually a percentage factor (i.e. 89.6%, 99.6%, etc.).

Paternity by Default[8]—When an alleged father fails to respond, or appear in court after being served in a paternity case, the court may issue a default judgment for paternity. This default judgment declares him as the father based on the court's satisfaction with whatever evidence is presented in accordance with that state's laws "upon a showing of service of process." This type of order is binding and is enforceable against the alleged father just as if he had been present at the hearing.

"Anyone who has a paternity declaration entered against him prior to October 1, 1995, without blood and genetic testing, generally may initiate proceedings to modify or set aside that declaration . . . ."
Langston v. Riffe, 754 Md. A.2d 389 (2000)

Establishment of Child Support Orders

The following are several processes used to establish support orders.

An *agreement* between two parties (CP and NCP), with the consent of both, can be used. However, when a CP is receiving state child support services, the court, or administrative authority may have to approve the terms to ensure that the agreement is beneficial for the child.

A *court hearing,* in which a case is heard and settled by judicial proceeding before a judge or administrative authority is also a common procedure used to establish a child support order. This includes divorce and other proceedings that enter a judgment for child support.

An *administrative hearing process* is similar to a court hearing. In this process a representative of the child support enforcement administration (usually an Administrative Law Judge) sets a hearing and presides over it to establish an order for support.

A Note on Gifts in Lieu of Child Support Payments . . .

Sometimes an NCP will give gifts, or do other special things for their child or children. While these gifts may be costly and go well beyond the amount of the support ordered obligation, it is important that you realize something. No matter how expensive these gifts are, they should not be considered as or take the place of your court ordered child support obligation. Unless you have some legal document instructing you to do so, you should avoid this practice.

By all means buy your children gifts, but know that gift giving is not a substitute for your legal obligation.

State Child Support Guideline Laws

States are required to use guidelines when establishing or modifying child support orders. However, in cases of extenuating circumstances when the amount computed using the guidelines would be "unjust or inappropriate in a particular case"[9] other measures are taken. Today's child support payment calculations must be "based on specific descriptive and numeric criteria." This is a big difference from the child support award days when "non-economic factors[10]" were generally used to determine the amount of child support an NCP would pay.

In some cases the guidelines calculations may produce a support obligation amount that "would be unjust or inappropriate in a particular case[11]." In these cases states have special circumstances that they consider sufficient to bypass the calculated support obligation. However, it should be noted that the existence of a particular circumstance or set of circumstances does not necessarily mean that guideline calculations will not, or should not be used. This section of guideline laws are nonetheless helpful when or if a court or administrative authority is considering whether or not to use the guidelines.

Each state's guidelines are reviewed and may be subject to change every four years "to ensure that their application results in the determination of appropriate child support award amounts[12]." For example, Georgia's current child support guidelines took effect in January of 2007. The old guidelines are based on the gross income of the NCP ONLY and did not take into account the CPs income. The amount of the child support obligation was determined by a sliding percentage scale that was based on the number of children for which support would be provided [13] (i.e. one child = 17%-23%, two children=23%-28%, three children=25%-32% and so on).

In addition to other revisions, Georgia's Child Support Guidelines now use an "Income Shares Model" formula where the support amount is based on both the NCP and CP incomes[14]. When this law became effective there was no automatic adjustment of child support obligations. NCPs in this state must show that the new formula would produce a minimum 15% change in their current obligation before any adjustment will be granted.

Some states like Texas and California may amend their guidelines more often due to the volume of cases they handle. State guidelines are always subject to change and it is up to the NCP to keep up with these changes and how they may affect your situation. You should log onto your state's child support website at least once a year to see if there has been any change that may affect your obligation.

Because a support obligation is based on "specific descriptive numeric criteria," an income amount must be used to calculate the amount of an obligation. When there is no income, states may impute it. A report from the Office of the Inspector General stated:

> Most states impute (i.e. attribute) income to the [NCP] if the [NCP] is unemployed or underemployed . . . . thirty-five states base imputed income on the premise that the [NCP] should be able to work a minimum wage job for 40 hours a week[15].

On the other hand, some states may use an NCP's earnings *potential* based on education, past work experience, or earnings history to impute income. If the occupation and earnings history are unknown, a state's average wage may be used. Exactly what factors and procedures go into each state's determination of whether or not an NCP has in fact voluntarily underemployed or unemployed themselves varies. It should be noted that whenever an NCP does voluntarily under-employ or unemploy him/herself by terminating a position with higher pay for one with less pay, it will always raise suspicion.

"*Person to whom income is to be imputed is entitled to an evidentiary hearing.*" **Pettit v Pettit, 612 N.E.2d 1090 (Ind. Ct. App. 1993)**

"*Earning capacity must be based on the ability as well as the opportunity to work.*" **Oregon v. Vargas, 70 Cal. App.4th 1123, 83 Cal. Rptr. 2d 229 (1999)**

Retroactive Support

Some states may limit retroactive support payments to the date the initial complaint was filed to request an order for support. In the case of existing orders, some states limit retroactive support to the date the application was filed requesting a modification, while other states may not. There are states which use their discretion in setting retroactive support to 12 months or more, prior to the date of any modification filed.

In my experience procedures not only differ from state to state on issues of retroactive support, but between welfare and non-welfare cases also. For example, in welfare cases, generally states charge NCPs for benefits paid to the CP and child prior to establishing an order. I have to pause here for a moment to share a thought that occurred to me years ago. My thought is this . . . if the NCP has no legal obligation to support the CP, to demand reimbursement from that NCP for the portion of benefits received by the CP is a fundamentally unfair practice. Moving on. There are also other charges which might include, but are not limited to court and attorney fees, case processing fees, charges for paternity testing, reimbursement of birth-related medical expenses, and other benefits paid by the state. Some or all of these charges are usually incorporated into an order, which is why many NCP's new support orders may begin with arrears.

As far as non-welfare cases are concerned, there is generally "no retroactive support," unless there was some prior divorce decree, separation agreement, or other instrument containing a provision for child support upon which to base the retroactive payment amount. Other than that, the date of the filing of the initial petition in a non-welfare case is usually the date of its effect. As far as arrears are concerned, there are procedures to "prohibit the retroactive modification of child support arrears by the state[16]."

Emancipation

The age of majority is 18 years of age in most states. However, there are states with a legal emancipation age of 21. In either case, some NCPs are responsible for financially supporting their children beyond the legal age of majority. These are usually in instances where there is a written agreement such as a separation or divorce decree stating such. There are also cases wherein a court may order financial support beyond the age of majority due to extenuating circumstances and/or the needs of the child.

In some cases where there are two or more children by the same CP and NCP, one of the children reaching 18 years of age does not necessarily mean that support payments can automatically be reduced. For example, I assisted in a case once where the order stated that a lump sum payment amount was to be paid instead of a specified amount to be paid "per child". The lump sum amount had to be paid, until the youngest child reached the age of majority, or was otherwise emancipated. I was informed that this matter depends on the specific language outlined in the order as well as the laws of that state.

If you are unsure of what your order states, you may want to have it reviewed by an attorney, especially if the case involves more than one child under the same order.

Paternal or Maternal Grandparent Support

If the NCP and CP are minors and the CP receives public assistance benefits for the child, if there is a court order for support, that order is enforceable (jointly and severally) against the parents of the minor NCP [17].

Medical Support Orders

Medical support is considered a form of child support. Therefore, "the law now requires employers to honor medical support orders established under state law[18]." Because of this, an order "may provide for specific dollar amounts to be deducted for medical purposes[19]", or a separate medical order may be established for this purpose. Health insurance is considered to be at "reasonable cost if provided through an employer or other group health insurance carrier" and (when available) the child support enforcement agency or court may require that an NCP provide this coverage for their dependent children[20]."

Where there has been an assignment of rights to the state, if the children do not have health insurance coverage (other than Medicaid), and the current order does not provide for it, a modification of the order may be made to include health insurance coverage. In this case a separate medical support order may be established. When there is an "assignment," this can be done regardless of whether or not health insurance is immediately available or available at a reasonable cost to the NCP[21].

Health insurance is considered reasonable if the cost to the providing parent does not exceed 5% of their gross income or at state option a reasonable alternative[22]. In some states when the CP has a health insurance plan that includes the children, the monthly premium already being paid by the CP is divided so that half of that total premium is included in the NCP's monthly support obligation. If both parents have plans that already cover the children, no additional amount is usually required to be paid by the NCP. Again this depends on the practice of your particular state.

Visitation

There are NCPs who believe that if the CP refuses to allow access to the child or children, the NCP has the right to withhold support. This is not true! There are also NCPs who believe the child support enforcement administration can help establish visitation rights. This is not true! Visitation and child support are two separate issues. The federal government offers grants for states to help establish Access and Visitation Programs to help NCPs struggling with visitation and other similar issues. You can log onto the child support website for your state for details on these programs.

If you are an NCP that does have access to and visitation with your child, you should be exercising your visitation rights by spending time with your child.

While visitation is not addressed by the child support enforcement agency, the amount of your visitation can have an impact on the amount of your child support obligation.

In some states joint custody, shared physical custody, divided custody, or multiple family adjustments are generally considered in setting or modifying a support obligation.

General or Standard visitation is typically 72 to 73 days; every other weekend (52), two weeks in summer (14), alternate Mother or Father's Day (1), Thanksgiving or Christmas (2), birthdays (1), and perhaps (2-3) extra days for a special event, program, outing, family reunion, etc. When the visitation that an NCP has with their child goes beyond general visitation, this often results in deviation from the guideline formula. How great that deviation is depends on the state and the discretion of the court. As well, exercising of these arrangements on part of the NCP matters to the courts and is taken into consideration. So, it is not enough to just have it in writing. NCPs should be making the most of their visitation and custody privileges, building and maintaining a relationship with their child or children.

Let's take a closer look at *shared physical custody* for a moment. As with most administrative practices, one state may regard shared physical custody differently than another state. For example, Alaska's definition is "a parent has shared physical custody (or shared custody) of the children for purposes of this rule if the children reside with that parent for a period specified in writing in the custody order of at least 30%, but no more than 70% of the year, regardless of the status of legal custody [23]," Whereas Maryland's definition is that "each parent keeps the child or children overnight for more than 35% of the year and that both parents contribute to the expenses of the child or children in addition to the payment of child support[24]." Either of these states may base a child support award obligation for shared physical custody on the amount of visitation awarded regardless of whether joint custody has actually been granted.

It is the NCP's responsibly to see that the issue of visitation is addressed (if applicable in their case) before the order is established. In the event that the issue was not addressed prior, and if the amount of visitation is significant, an NCP may want to seek a modification (see Chapter 5: Modifications).

REFERENCED IN THIS CHAPTER

1. 42 USC 666 (a)(5)(A)(i) (2010)
2. 42 USC 666 (a)(5)(ii)(iii) (2010)
3. 42 USC 666 (a)(5)(D)(iii) (2010)
4. 42 USC 666 (a)(5)(C)(i) (2010)
5. CLASP (Center for Law and Social Policy) Re: Update on the Uniform Parentage Act (2010)
6. 42 USC 666 (a)(5)(B)(i) (2010)
7. 42 USC 666 (a)(5)(G) (2010)
8. 42 USC 666(a)(5)(H) (2010)
9. 45 CFR 302.56(a), (g) (2010).
10. 45 CFR 302.56 (c)(2) (2010)
11. 45 CFR 302.56(g) (2005)
12. 45 CFR 302.56(e) (2010).
13. OCGA 19-6-15
14. House Bill 221
15. *June Gibbs Brown, US DHHS Office of Inspector General, State Policies Used to Establish Child Support Orders for Low Income Non-custodial Parents, OEI, July 2000.*
16. 42 USC 666 (a)(9)(C) (2009)
17. 42 USC 666 (a)(18) (2010)
18. The ABC's of Child Support Employer Overview Packet—Medical Support Insert.
19. The ABC's of Child Support Employer Overview Packet—Medical Support Insert.
20. The ABC's of Child Support Employer Overview Packet—Medical Support Insert.

21. 45 CFR 303.31 (b) (1),(2) (i) (ii) (2009)
22. 45 CFR 303.31 (a) (3) (b) (1),(2),(3) (i),(ii) (2010)
23. Alaska Rule 90.3(f) (1) 2009.
24. Annotated Code of Md.12-202(i) (1) 2009.

CHAPTER 3

The Importance of Case Monitoring & Payment Tracking

I have found that most NCPs monitor their bank accounts more closely than they monitor their child support payments. This simply should not be! We obviously do not just assume that everything our bank does with our account is accurate. Otherwise, we would not bother to reconcile our bank statement each month. Why do we take the time to do something so tedious and boring? Because we know that everyone and everything is prone to error.

Have you ever considered what it means to reconcile? According to Merriam-Webster's Dictionary, in this instance it means "to check a financial account against another for accuracy." My suggestions and recommendations do not really differ from this core concept. You should be *checking* a financial account, (*the child support agency's record* of your account) *against* another (*your personal records* and payment receipts). Why? To ensure ACCURACY, that's why.

It is appropriate then, that I introduce to you to two concepts with which you should become thoroughly familiar: *case monitoring* and *payment tracking*. While they are very similar, there are some minor differences in their meanings which you should know.

What Are Case Monitoring & Payment Tracking? How Do They Work?

Case monitoring is a process in which you periodically compare your personal child support case information to the agency's information to verify that they both are accurate.

Payment tracking is a process in which you personally maintain accurate records of all child support payments made in your case, to be compared later to those of the child support enforcement agency for *accuracy*.

In order to conduct proper *Case Monitoring* you will need the following for each case you have:

- Your account number with the child support enforcement agency
- File and/or Docket # (if applicable)
- CP/Payee's full name and address
- Your social security number
- Copies of the support order, including any modified orders
- Names, ages and birth dates of each of your children and social security numbers for health insurance and other purposes

- Address of the child support enforcement agency (or agencies) that handle your case(s)
- Your caseworker's name and phone number for the local agency that handles your case

Note: If you have an out-of-state child support case, you need to make sure that you have case information regarding your case with that agency also.

The following case is a perfect example of how beneficial case monitoring and payment tracking could have been for this NCP.

How to Monitor Your Child Support Case

Make notes of important dates: when your children are to be emancipated, when there is to be an increase or decrease in your ordered obligation (if applicable), and other important events regarding your child support case. Always verify the following information on any document(s) you receive pertaining to your child support case.

- Correct spelling of name(s) for you, the CP, and the children
- Social Security numbers
- Child support agency's account numbers
- The agency name and address on the documents you received
- Case numbers (court system's filing/docket number and agency case number)
- Type of case (TANF, FC or NON-AFDC/ NTANF)

- The state that issued or forwarded the correspondence
- Amount of court ordered obligation
- Amount of arrears
- Date(s)

If you have more than one child support case, be sure the information you receive is the correct information *for that case*, and does not include mixed information from any other case.

These areas are the focal points for verification. However, if anything else appears questionable, verify that information as well. If you notice an error, contact your caseworker immediately. If the information checks out, file it away. Keep a record of any adjustments or corrections made in your case.

Case Summary #1

Occupation: Custodian
Problem: Unknown at time of initial case investigation
Alleged Arrears: $13,000

Mr. Anderson was paying child support by wage garnishment, which included payments toward arrears. Mr. Anderson's son for whom these arrears were said to be due was in his mid-twenties at this time. According to Mr. Anderson, the local child support enforcement agency said he owed an estimated $13,000 in arrears for reimbursement of welfare the CP and child had received years ago.

Initially, Mr. Anderson did not think he had a problem. He said, "Why would they make me pay it if I didn't owe

---

it?" Meanwhile, the agency that had been handling Mr. Anderson's taxes for years noticed that something was not quite right. Of special interest was the number of Mr. Anderson's tax refunds that were taken year after year. Concerned, the tax preparer informed Mr. Anderson that he suspected something was not right, but he did not know what. The tax preparer, who was familiar with my work on similar cases, contacted me on Mr. Anderson's behalf. After meeting with him I agreed to take the case.

Findings:

I found that Mr. Anderson was in fact in arrears at one time. However, those arrears had been satisfied four years prior to the start of my investigation. As for the wage garnishment, it had been issued for current support. This made no sense because the minor in question had been emancipated years earlier. The order had been issued years after that state's statute of limitations for establishing an order. The earnings withholding order was totally improper to begin with. The obligation of support based on this order was not Mr. Anderson's in the first place. It was meant for his son.

Apparently, Mr. Anderson's son, Mr. Anderson, Jr., had himself fathered a child that he had no knowledge of. Judging from the reaction of Mr. Anderson, Sr., he didn't know anything about the child either. The agency's explanation was that there was probably some sort of mix up in the names because the older Mr. Anderson never used "Sr." after his name. Apparently no one in the agency thought to check or double check the social security numbers for the men either. If they had done so they would have realized that the order had been issued for Mr. Anderson, Jr. rather than for Mr. Anderson, Sr.

Results:

Needless to say, the case of Mr. Anderson, Sr. was closed, and the necessary steps were taken to establish a case for his son. Although Mr. Anderson Sr., never received a letter of apology from the administration, he did receive reimbursements of over $6,000 for the tax refunds that were intercepted in addition to reimbursements of payments made by wage garnishment. BELIEVE IT OR NOT!

How to Do Payment Tracking

To start, I suggest that you request a copy of your child support payment history from your local child support enforcement agency *at least once a year.* This information will likely be more detailed than what you would typically receive from the State Disbursement Unit (SDU). Many states provide customer/client portals where you can access customer service/support immediately via the internet. I recommend requesting this information at the end of February following the year you are tracking. That way, all payments made through December of the previous year should be posted. While some states may allow you to access this information online, it still may be a good idea to make an appointment to have your caseworker review the payment history with you, as sometimes these reports can be quite intimidating.

Total all of your payments made to each case separately. If you had tax-refund interceptions, or other types of interceptions, include these amounts in your calculation of payments.

When you receive your payment record, compare your full-year payment receipt total to the agency's full-year payment record total, paying close attention to the arrears. If there is a conflict in those amounts, double-check the totals. If the figures still do not match, contact your caseworker as soon as possible for a review of your case.

To maintain proper records, you must create an organizational system. Simply use a small box, container, or large envelope to hold your receipts for safekeeping. Mark it "Child Support Information" (or something similar). If you are paying by wage garnishment, when payday comes, *do not* shove your pay stubs in the glove compartment, or the armrest of the car. Keep them in your wallet or your pocket. At the end of your workday empty your pockets, and put your pay stubs in the place you have chosen for safekeeping. At the end of the month, clip or band them together until it is time to reconcile your receipts with the agency's records at the end of the year. Do the same thing for any other type of child support payment receipts you may have. If your tax refund is intercepted keep proof of that as well.

Note: If you have arrears, and you are making payments toward those arrears, be sure that those payments are reflected in your payment records, and that the amount of those arrears is continuously being reduced in the agency's payment report.

Case Summary #2

Occupation: Bus Driver

Problem: Wanted to know if alleged arrears were true

Alleged Arrears: $32,000

Mr. G was not aware of any current support order, but indicated that he had had a wage garnishment years prior which lasted for about four or five years. He also indicated that he'd had several tax refund interceptions and was being charged with more than $17,000 in arrears for reimbursement to the state, and $15,000 in arrears to the CP for past due support. He wanted an investigation conducted to see how much more money he owed in back support. If he had kept a copy of his court order, and clearly understood it, this entire situation could have been avoided, or, at the very least, could have been addressed long before it was.

Findings:

Originally there was an order filed that was only to run for three years. That order stayed active longer than it should have. When the wage garnishment eventually did stop, the provisions outlined in the order went unnoticed. As a result, the amount due continued to accumulate as if it were unpaid current support. This qualified Mr. G for tax refund interception for what appeared as non-payment of his support obligation. This illustrates that careful reading and understanding of the provisions outlined in a court order are crucial. This NCP should have contacted the local child support enforcement agency to inquire about the court order and the arrears as soon as he was notified that he had them. He should have kept track of his child support payments. Then he would have known for certain that the arrearage amount was incorrect. Personal case monitoring would have uncovered the error, and payment tracking would have identified the overpayment and reflected the overcharge in the amount being requested.

Results:

All arrears were abated and Mr. G's name was removed from the tax-refund certification list. Overpayment was found and refunded to the NCP of over $3,200 in one check and an undisclosed amount in another check. Current support was suspended and the case was closed retroactive to the date of the youngest son's 18th birthday, six years prior. Correct amount of arrears in this case: $0.

Tips for Effective Case Monitoring & Payment Tracking

- If you have problems understanding something about your child support case, ASK QUESTIONS!
- If you have more than one child support case, remember to keep the information regarding each case separate.
- Store your support order and other important documents pertaining to your case in a SAFE place.
- Always inquire about a matter regarding your case if ANYTHING at all appears questionable.
- Request a copy of your payment history from the agency AT LEAST ONCE A YEAR.
- Set a tentative time to do your annual payment tracking. I strongly suggest TAX PREPARATION TIME each year.

- ALWAYS honor the instructions outlined in your court order.
- NEVER throw away payment receipts, pay stubs, etc., or leave them scattered about. Keep them in a SAFE place.
- NEVER throw away any letter, document or other mail you receive from the child support enforcement agency or others regarding your case. You may need them later.
- NEVER assume that your child support caseworker is aware of a specific problem or situation if you have not discussed it with him or her yourself.
- NEVER disregard an issue relating to your case if you suspect there is a problem.
- NEVER give cash payment without some sort of receipt, if you intend to regard those cash payments as a means of support. More importantly, you should always make payments through the agency when instructed to do so.
- If you have more than one child support case ALWAYS keep track of the same information for each one (i.e. case numbers, social security numbers, payments, etc.) and again, keep case information separate.
- READ DOCUMENTS BEFORE YOU SIGN THEM! Be sure that you fully understand what you are signing. If you are not clear about something you would do well to seek the advice of an attorney. Paying the cost of consultation, or representation if needed, could prove less expensive than the price you may have to pay later to correct a matter.

Making a decision to personally monitor your child support case is very advantageous and empowering. Besides, what have you got to lose?

Case Summary #3

Occupation: Construction Worker

Problem: Suspected Overpayment of Obligation

Alleged Arrears: Over $2,000

Mr. William had received tax-refund interceptions for more than three years, and paid current support by wage garnishment, which included payment toward arrears. The local child support enforcement agency said that he owed arrears of over $2,000. He disagreed, but he failed to address it at the time, behavior typical of many NCPs.

Findings:

The NCP had overpayments to both the CP and the state. However, child support enforcement agencies *do not* seek reimbursement of overpayment from the CP. The NCP first suspected a problem two years prior when $175 of his tax refund was intercepted, but it was not until the amount was too much to ignore that he decided to get help. He should have been on the case when he first suspected he had an overpayment. He should not have waited!

Results:

The correct arrearage due in this case was $403. Credit for overpayment was applied to the NCPs account, and a $487 reimbursement was paid to the NCP from additional overpayment previously held by the state.

Undistributed Collections

In Chapter 1, I briefly touched on the subject of undistributed collections. In this chapter I will go into more detail. It is my sincere hope that you will begin to see the child support payments you make in a different light, if you have not already.

Undistributed collections (UDC) are child support payments received by state child support enforcement agencies that have not been distributed and/or disbursed. As an NCP or CP for that matter—this should concern you, because the child support payments that fall into the UDC category will likely be escheated to the state as abandoned property. States are federally required to report abandoned property (including child support payments) to the federal government. The good news is that there are several types of payments that may fall under state's UDC categories that you may be able to get out of UDC status before they are escheated to the state as abandoned property. I have listed five UDC payment categories[1], a description of each and my suggestions for prevention and/or correction.

UDC Categories, descriptions and suggestions on avoiding them.

Category #1: Unidentified Collection
Description: Payments received by the state that cannot be properly allocated because the case to which it belongs cannot be identified.

Suggestion(s): Be sure that every payment made to your case has the correct case name and account number on it. If you have a wage lien, see to it that your employer includes all of the pertinent information required for each of those payments as well, especially for electronic payments. These types of payments generally have a case identifier number that may differ from the regular agency case number.

Category #2: Held Pending Location of CP or NCP
Description: Payments collected by a state that were allocated to the proper case, but the whereabouts of the intended payee is unknown. These payments include payments to CPs as well as refunds an NCP is entitled to.
Suggestion(s): Be sure to keep current information on file with the agency for yourself, especially as you near the end of your support obligation. When possible, encourage the CP to give a forwarding address to the child support agency if they move. Properly monitor your case and pay close attention to payments you make toward arrears. When those arrears are satisfied, if the agency has not reduced your obligation by that amount, contact them. Be aware of any overpayment that may be accumulating while you are waiting for this issue to be resolved. If you have to pay child support you should ensure that your child benefits from it.

Category #3: Uncashed/Stale Dated
Description: Payments collected by a state and properly disbursed to CPs or refunded to the NCP in the form of a check that was never cashed by the recipient and is now no longer valid.

Suggestion(s): This is a preventable problem that the CP should address. Again, make sure that **you** keep **your** information current and encourage the CP to do so when possible. These payments are said to be redistributed before they are re-categorized as a "hold pending location of CP or NCP" prior to being escheated to the state as abandoned property.

Category #4: Inaccurate or Missing Information
Description: Payment collections that are received by the state and allocated to a specific case but cannot be disbursed because case information included with the payment is inaccurate, missing the proper amount, or the amount of the payment does not match the stated transmittal amount. Or perhaps, the payment has been received for a case that is no longer open or active.
Suggestion(s): Be sure that your payments have current and accurate information (i.e. name, case number and payment amount) and that the case is still active. Know when your support obligation is to end so that you do not have more payments than required being credited (or attempting) to be credited to an inactive or closed account.

Category #5: Other Collections
Description: This is the default UDC category when payments do not fit one of the other four categories.
Suggestion(s): Be sure that every payment made to your case has the correct case name and account number on it. And, that every payment you make is accounted for and has been properly distributed.
The payments that find their way into the five categories mentioned above will remain there until:

case identification is possible, the payee or payor is located, a reliable address is found, all pertinent information becomes available or until they inevitably "meet the state criteria to be escheated as 'abandoned property[2].'"

How You Can Protect Your Child Support Investment

Effective Case Monitoring and Payment Tracking are essential and the two most important things that you can do to ensure that the payments you make to your case are properly credited to your account, and not escheated to the state as abandoned property. The sooner you become more proactive in your case the greater the benefit. Some state systems are set up to automatically transfer payments to the abandoned property collection account after being held in UDC status for anywhere from 90 days to 180 days depending on the UDC category. The sooner you begin monitoring the better. You should also check with the unclaimed property office in your state. Conducting a missing money search with your state's unclaimed property department is not a bad idea either.

REFERENCED IN THIS CHAPTER

[1 & 2] OCSE-AT-04-07 September 30, 2004 Section A.

CHAPTER 4

Addressing Your Local Child Support Enforcement Agency

A Note about Customer Service Relations

For over twenty years, I have assisted many NCPs with problematic child support cases. During that time, I've observed that most NCPs complain about the lack of interest caseworkers, customer service representatives and/or agents show when dealing with issues that do not relate to enforcement or collection of support payments.

For the most part, I agree. Yes, child support matters are complex, difficult and intimidating at times, and solutions are generally not "one size fits all." Therefore, some frustration is to be expected. However, NCPs who are rude or belligerent should not be surprised if they receive less than courteous service from their caseworkers, customer service representatives or child support enforcement agents.

The caseworkers with whom I have dealt have been very pleasant and helpful. However, I do realize that everyone has not had such experiences. In fact, many of the NCPs I have assisted have spoken of their rather unpleasant experiences with caseworkers, and have referred to them as the "enemy." Despite that, and contrary to popular belief, your child support enforcement agent/caseworker is not the enemy. They are people with a job to do, just like you.

Granted, you may find some that are a bit edgy or even a bit curt when dealing with you, but consider their position. Caseworkers juggle hundreds of cases. Each of those cases represents *at least* two people, you and the other parent. On any given day your caseworker might receive as many as 100 calls, if not more. A good percentage of these callers are disgruntled. So, you should not be surprised if from time to time your caseworker does not greet you with all the tact and pleasantness of Mary Poppins or Mr. Rogers. I am not by any means laying the responsibility for the quality of customer service in the laps of NCPs. However, you should be aware that the actions of some make things worse for the next person.

On the other hand there is no excuse for a caseworker, child support enforcement agent/customer service representative, or other who displays rudeness, disrespect, or indifference. I have witnessed jaded and weary caseworkers who on more than one occasion have labeled *any* NCP who has arrears a "deadbeat". To this, I have but one thing to say: cases represent *people,* and people should be dealt with selectively as individuals, and not collectively, as a group.

Filing a Complaint

How you go about making complaints to the child support agency may vary from one state to the next. However, all states must have some form of administrative complaint procedures in place that will afford you the opportunity to request action when there is evidence of an error or problem with your case[38]. States are required to make these procedures known to all individuals receiving service.

Scenario A

You receive a letter from the agency about arrears that you owe. Or, maybe you receive a call from your child's other parent about payments not being received. In any event you will need to contact the agency about the matter. Do this immediately!

> **Tip:** When you are notified of a situation, whether it be by the agency or the other parent in your case take a minute to figure out what could have happened to create the situation, or what may have been a contributing factor to it. Ask yourself questions regarding the situation. Did I miss any payments? Was there a change in employment? If so, when? And so on.

When an error or oversight occurs through no fault of your own, even if it truly is an administrative error, *you should never regard it as "just an administrative error."* Doing so could lead you to believe that you are not accountable for the resulting problem, thereby giving you the impression that because the error was not your fault it makes it someone else's problem, not yours. **BIG MISTAKE!** If you are the one with the obligation of support *anything* that affects your case makes it YOUR PROBLEM.

Scenario B

You send in a support payment, and it does not show in your payment report. Who is responsible for *proof* of that payment? You are! If your tax refund was intercepted and that payment does not show in your payment report, who is responsible for *proof* of that payment by interception? You are! Now, if you are able to show *proof* of payment it becomes clear that it was in fact an administrative error or oversight. Remember, if payments are missing, the burden of proof rests on you. YOUR payment record is flawed and YOUR CHILD misses a payment. Even though it may have been an "administrative error or oversight," you are the responsible party.

What an NCP must do in any situation like this is contact the local child support enforcement agency that holds their case. Following are the various ways to do so most effectively.

Inquiry by Phone . . .

Most caseworkers have special times during which they receive phone calls. Know what the schedule is. Use it.

- Be prepared to give your caseworker or customer-service agent the necessary case information.
- Make a note of the date and the person with whom you spoke.
- If you are asked to call back for a follow up, do so.
- Be specific regarding the nature of your call. Simply state the facts.
- If the agency does not respond within a reasonable time (est. 10-15 days), contact that state's child support enforcement administration. They should have access to the same information.

Inquiry by Letter . . .

This form of inquiry is often a better method of communication because it gives you documented proof of your inquiry. It is especially helpful when notifying the agency of important changes (i.e. change of employer, relocation, etc.). As with inquiry by phone, be specific. Many agencies have their own standard inquiry forms, and most of them come with instructions. You may want to look into that. If they do not have their own forms, you may want to try composing a simple letter.

Your letter of inquiry or any other correspondence should always contain the following information:

- Your full name, current address and telephone number (include the best time to reach you.)
- Your social security number

- Name of CP and Child
- Correct account number. If you do not know your account numbers ask your caseworker for it and make a note of it.
- Your caseworker's name (if applicable)
- Date of your letter
- Reason for inquiry (stated briefly)

The following is a sample letter in its simplest form from a Mr. John Q. Payor.

~~~~~~

John Q. Payor
1234 Any Road
Any City, Any State 01234
(000) 555-1111 (Best Time: after 3:00)

Local Child Support Agency
Attn: Mr. Case
5678 Enforcement Blvd.
Any City, Any State 56789

October 01, 2010
RE: Case Name: CP vs NCP
Acct.#: 7777777
SS#: 888-88-8888
Child: John Payor Jr.

Dear Mr. Brown:

I received a letter stating that I owe $800 in arrears. I believe this is incorrect. Please send me a copy of my payment history reflecting which payments are missing. I will compare my receipts. If there is an error, I will contact you for a review of my case.

Sincerely,

John Q. Payor

~~~~~~

You will notice that this letter is brief, yet it contains all the necessary pieces of information required for a proper response. Be sure you have the correct address for the child support enforcement agency that handles your case. Always address your inquiry directly to your caseworker, if possible.

In some states the full name of the caseworker is not divulged. Some agencies also have customer service agents to provide needed assistance. Whatever your agency's policies, try to find a person to whom you can direct your inquiry. It is not a prudent practice to address a letter, "To Whom It May Concern."

You may also want to call your caseworker ahead of time so that he or she will be expecting your letter. Allow at least two weeks for a response. If you have not received the response by then, you may want to do a follow-up call.

Inquiry by Fax & E-Mail . . .

These two methods are a quick way to make an inquiry. However, they may not be the most effective. All agencies may not be prepared to receive an influx of faxes, and e-mails. On the other hand, some agencies may prefer this method as opposed to telephone calls. I suggest you contact that local child support enforcement agency to be sure if either of these is acceptable before wasting your time. Remember that in many states, case information can be accessed online.

In-Person Conferences . . .

Say you are dealing with the previous scenario we used, but you feel strongly that you need to see your caseworker in person to resolve the matter.

The very first thing you should do is call to schedule an appointment. Drop-ins are not usually very effective even when they are allowed. In most cases, proper time to research information is usually necessary to resolve a matter. Caseworkers are busy people, so it is important to know that you may be waiting awhile if you do decide to just drop in. After a long day at work I am sure you would not appreciate a long wait at the child support enforcement agency. So, call first!

When you do go in, have your paperwork in order, especially if your visit is in regard to miscalculation or omission of payments. Organize your documents! Do not just bring in a bag of unorganized receipts. Your caseworker will not spend 30 minutes of an estimated one-hour appointment (if that long) sorting through a mess, only to find that accurate calculation is not possible because most of the receipts are missing. This may sound funny, but it happens. So, do yourself a favor—organize them!

Out of State Court or Administrative Hearings

When you (an NCP) are summoned to testify for hearing or are requesting a hearing and you live out of state, you can usually request the court or administration's permission to testify by telephonic, audio-visual or other means. If you find it necessary to do this, you should be sure to keep the scheduled hearing time as promptly as you would if you appeared in person before the court or administration for a formal hearing. Telephonic hearings are just as serious as formal hearings. It is always good to have an attorney to represent you in these matters, but if counsel does not represent you it would be prudent for you to seek out some sort of legal advice beforehand rather than going it alone.

Make sure that you have chosen an appropriate place in which to hold the telephonic hearing. Be sure that you have a working telephone and that the telephone number given to the court for the hearing is a number for a landline (conventional phone) and not a cell phone. You do not want to lose a signal or have your call drop right in the middle of your hearing. The court or administration should give you an itemized list of what documents you need to submit to the court ahead of time. If they do not offer to provide you this information, ask them for it. You should also send any information requested by the out of state court by certified mail requiring a signature at delivery. Keep this information for your records.

Teamwork

If while reading this chapter you get the idea that I am promoting some sort of "*Teamwork*", you have perceived correctly! Now, that may seem a little farfetched in matters pertaining to child support enforcement, but that is really how it is. An associate of mine said that "Teamwork is best described as united effort/efficient cooperation" and I agree. I'll show you what I mean using Scenario B, again.

You send a payment in, and the agency has no record of it. There is a hang-up somewhere. Therefore, between *you,* and *your caseworker* (united effort) you need to find out what happened. If your caseworker cannot find the payment you should be able to provide the proof needed to correct the error (efficiency). By working with your caseworker in providing that proof (cooperation), your account is updated, the error is corrected, and your caseworker gets to lighten the problem caseload by one file. So you see, helping your caseworker helped you. More importantly, your child benefited. After all, your child cannot get a payment if the records do not reflect it.

So, like it or not, teamwork is what it is! You do not have to invite your caseworker over for coffee, or do lunch, but there should be a level of cooperation and mutual respect between both parties.

No matter what, NCPs have got to start speaking up and interacting more effectively in regard to their cases. You should be asking questions, doing your own research and reading everything before you sign any document relating to your case.

CHAPTER 5

Modifications

A *modification* is a change in your support order, upon review and adjustments. In non-welfare cases, a review to modify an order must be at the request of either the CP or NCP. Also, a state-assessed fee may be required of the requesting party. In welfare cases, the state conduct reviews on a regular basis without a request from either party[1]. States' review periods differ and may be every two years. In any case, it is mandatory for states to have procedures for reviewing, adjusting, and challenging any proposed adjustments or determinations in place for all child support cases.

While these modifications are generally performed by the agency or requested by the CP or NCP every three years, a case may be modified sooner to decrease as well as increase current support[2]. In this case, the person requesting the modification must show proof of change in circumstances. The qualifying factors for these changes in circumstances vary among states.

You should know that some states will not consider a modification to decrease, or increase an order unless that change totals at least 25% upward or downward of the current support obligation, whereas others allow for modifications at an amount of only 5% or 10% upward or downward of the current support obligation. Orders may also be modified to include health insurance.

In cases where an order of modification is granted, an NCP will likely incur arrears even if the NCP had no prior arrears. Why? Generally, modified orders state that the new payment amount is to begin "retroactive" to the date the request for a modification was filed, not as of the date the modification was actually established as the new or current order. This unfortunately puts an NCP in arrears before they have even begun to meet their obligation.

Case Summary #4

Occupation: Contractor

Problem: NCP disagreed with amount of arrears; CP unknowingly was missing support payments, case needed to be modified. Parties in this case were not aware that they needed a modification.

Alleged Arrears: $20,000

An NCP has two separate child support cases open in the same state. None of the parties in either case had lived in that state for eight or nine years. In addition, one of the CPs had been his wife for the last four years. The arrears for his wife's case totaled over $20,000. The NCP had a wage garnishment for $125 per week. This was later increased to almost $190 per week, and included more than $60.00 toward the arrears. The NCP indicated that he was sure he had accumulated an arrearage from years past when he was unemployed due to a non-employment related injury, but

---

nothing like the amount the child support enforcement agency stated. This case involved a CP and NCP who had children, and later married. However, prior to their union the CP received welfare assistance. **Remember,** whenever there is involvement of welfare benefits paid to the CP on behalf of themselves and the children, the NCP is responsible for reimbursing the state for these payments once an order has been established. The fact that these two were married had no bearing on the amount of money the state said the NCP owed. However, the amount of time she received welfare and when they married does. Why? Support orders, like anything else, have a time-table (i.e. effective dates). Therefore, while events in and of themselves may not matter, the dates and places they occurred could.

Findings:
The state had an active child support case open for his wife as if she were still a current resident of that state and currently receiving welfare benefits. The other case had remained open and the whereabouts of the other CP and child were unknown by the state or the NCP at the time of this investigation. This couple should have sought help a lot sooner. Instead they left it alone as if the matter would simply just go away. Problems should be addressed not dismissed! *Food for thought:* This NCP could have benefited from monitoring his case as well as keeping track of the child support payments he had made. However, and more importantly, he should have notified the local child support enforcement agency when he first suspected that there was a problem.

Results:
Initially the child support enforcement agency made adjustments in the amount of arrears due the state as

reimbursement. This left the NCP with an adjusted arrearage amount of $9,675 (a difference of over $11,000). The active welfare case was closed, and current support was suspended. In addition, his wife received a lump sum payment that had originally been held by the state as reimbursement to welfare. The wage garnishment was reduced, but would stay in effect until the remaining arrears were satisfied.

States are required to give notice to CPs and NCPs (at least every 3 years) informing them of their right to request a review of their child support order[3]. It is not necessary to prove any change in circumstances to have a case reviewed every three years[4]. In Uniform Interstate Family Support Act (UIFSA) cases, "a state may only modify an order of another state under certain conditions[5]." The agency guides the parent in how the request should be made, and inform him/her that there may be costs associated with the request. Talk to your local agency. This will be discussed more in the next chapter.

A few situations that may warrant a modification include, but are not limited to . . .

- The CP losing physical custody of the child or children
- Substantial changes in income
- Change in needs of parent or child
- Extraordinary medical expenses of the child, CP or NCP
- Incarceration of CP or NCP

- Health-related (physical or mental) issues of custodial parent

Whenever a change in circumstance occurs regarding your child support case, you should never hesitate to contact the child support agency that handles your case.

The case that I am about to share with you is not your average case of a CP no longer having custody, but it is relevant just the same. My desire in sharing this case is more so for you to understand the importance of reporting issues in a timely matter and to give a small example of what another NCP faced for not being prompt in seeking assistance or the right answers. And just as importantly how he could have benefited from case monitoring and payment tracking.

Case Summary #5

Occupation: Retail Manager

Problem: NCP needed a modification and wanted to know what the accurate amount of arrears was.

Alleged Arrears: Over $17,000

A CP goes to prison and the NCP takes the children into his home. The NCP had *de facto* custody of his children for more than a year. However, because no order was ever filed giving him legal custody the child support agency would not recognize him as the CP and therefore refused to relieve him of his obligation of current support. The agency also stated that it could not make any adjustment to arrears that accrued once he took the children in, despite the fact that the biological mother had been in prison for

---

an unknown amount of time. The NCP was charged with more than $17,000 in child support arrears due the state as a reimbursement for welfare, and to the imprisoned CP. Neither the CP nor NCP notified the Department of Social Services of the situation so monthly benefits continued to be forwarded to the former residence of the CP and children. The NCP also failed to immediately inform the local child support enforcement agency of the situation which largely contributed to this problem. This situation could have been resolved a lot sooner, and long before the arrears reached the reported amount, had the NCP known what to do.

Findings:
The amount of arrears due the state as reimbursement for welfare was improper and miscalculated. This NCP always had a wage garnishment for this case. However, one of his previous employers went out of business years prior to this situation. Unfortunately, this NCP failed to keep better records of his child support payments. Therefore, he had no proof that payments were forwarded to the child support enforcement agency for that particular time period. Had he been able to provide proof of additional payments he had made, the remaining arrears would have been even less. Case monitoring and payment tracking would have greatly benefited this NCP.

Results:
The case was suspended for current support and adjustments made to the arrears. The proper amount of arrears due after adjustments was about $8,000 which was due the state prior to the NCP having physical custody of his children. This balance was said to have been negotiated for

settlement upon the NCPs payment of at least 50 percent of the remaining debt. We found out what information the administration needed as proof to verify the facts and change in circumstances (i.e. the children's school records which reflected the NCPs address not the CPs, etc.) Once all of the information was gathered it was forwarded to the local child support enforcement agency. Upon review, a conference was held, and the matter was resolved as stated above.

In cases where an NCP is incarcerated, they may be able to get a modification to have their support order changed or temporarily suspended during some or all of their incarceration, but they have to **file** for the modification.

REFERENCED IN THIS CHAPTER

[1] 42USC666(a)(10)(A)(i) (2009)
[2] 42 USC 666(a)(10)(B)
[3] 42 USC 666(a)(10)(C (2009)
[4] 42USC666(a)(10)(A)(iii) (2010)
[5] OCSE UIFSA Handbook

CHAPTER 6

Interstate Child Support

URESA/RURESA, UIFSA? What is it?

As odd sounding as they are, these acronyms are short for the names given to, and the laws governing, interstate child support orders. **URESA** is the acronym for *Uniform Reciprocal Enforcement of Support Act, and* the revised version of it is the **RURESA,** short for *Revised Uniform Reciprocal Enforcement of Support Act*. Lastly, there is **UIFSA** (*Uniform Interstate Family Support Act*) which has replaced both the URESA/RURESA[10].

Case Summary #6
Occupation: *Government Employee*
Problem: *More than one wage garnishment for the same CP and children*
Estimated Arrears: *over $14,900*

After his divorce, Mr. Brown relocated to another state. During this time he had a wage garnishment for his child support and spousal support totaling $518 per month. Two years after he relocated the local child support enforcement agency in his former state of residency filed an order

---

reducing his payments to $415 per month (relieving him of his spousal support obligation). We will refer to this agency as agency no.1. One year after that order was filed; Mr. Brown received a copy of a new order for $300 per month that was different than the previous orders in one way. This third order was a URESA Order (see Chapter Five). He assumed that the order had been changed because he and his ex-wife were living in different states, but did nothing to confirm that this was the case.

When Mr. Brown saw his paycheck he realized something was seriously wrong. Where there was once a $95.84 deduction per week ($415 per month), there was now a $165.13 deduction. What this meant was that in addition to the $415 per month payment for agency no. 1 he was now paying an additional support order of $300 per month to agency no. 2. Mr. Brown's new monthly deductions for child support now totaled over $700 per month for two separate orders for the same child support case.

Mr. Brown struggled for years to correct this situation. He also was not able to see his children during this time.

According to their records, before the end of that same year Mr. Brown had accumulated arrears to agency no.1 of over $4,600, and arrears to agency no.2 of over $7,300. As if he did not have enough problems, in December of the same year he received an interception notice from yet another agency in another state which we will refer to as agency no.3. This one was for over $3,000.

This situation went on for five-and-a-half years prior to my meeting with Mr. Brown. At that point he wanted any relief possible and just wanted to know what in the heck was going on. After an initial investigation to ensure that there was no domestic violence involved I agreed to investigate the case.

Findings:
Well, it seemed that Mr. Brown's ex-wife had been busy over the last five-and-a-half years. Busy packing! She had relocated to four different states in five years time, leaving a trail of state-assigned support rights everywhere she stopped. Mr. Brown was actually under four obligations for *three different states.* The first state, his former residence and home of agency no.1, had him under one order. The second state, the first home of his ex-wife and home of agency no.2, had him under a second order. A third state agency placed him under an additional order when his ex-wife relocated there. The fourth state—where Mr. Brown actually lived—was acting on URESA Orders from agencies no. 1 and no. 2.

What made this case so unbelievable, at least to me, was that none of the three states had knowledge that the others were acting on orders for the same CP and children! In fact, two of these states assumed that the CP and children were still residing there. I found that the CP failed to inform any of the agencies involved that she had in fact relocated, which left open welfare cases for her in three states. Because the cases were never closed, Mr. Brown continued to incur arrearages for those states.

Results:
After communication was established between the four states, adjustments were made to Mr. Brown's cases within

their agencies, and the appropriate cases were closed. His wages continued to be garnished, but now it was for the amount of his actual obligation. Mr. Brown's payments were sent through his local child support enforcement agency for appropriate distribution. It turned out that Mr. Brown's actual arrears were less than $2,000. They were reduced even further because of direct payments Mr. Brown had made previously by wire transfers that were not credited to his account. In addition, he finally got to see his children after almost six years. BELIEVE IT OR NOT!

States were allowed to adopt portions of URESA creating complications with multiple orders for an individual case *(i.e. Case Summary #6 above)*. Problems like this brought about the creation of UIFSA, which requires uniformity across states. As such, UIFSA focuses on establishment, modification, and enforcement of child support orders. It has standard rules, procedures, and even the necessary forms to be used for interstate cases. This way, parents are subjected to only one order for an individual case at one time.

While UIFSA has replaced URESA, all states had not adopted UIFSA at the time I began researching this subject. According to sources who work directly in this field, even if all states had adopted it, it would still be quite some time (years) before URESA orders are worked completely out of the system. For that reason, I thought it would be a good idea to broaden the scope of information provided on these acts as they are set out in the Office of Child Support Enforcement UIFSA Handbook.

Let's begin with a few terms and definitions used in the UIFSA cycle as well as some other information. These are summaries, not comprehensive definitions.

Term	Definition
Home State	Refers to the state where the child lived with a parent or person acting as parent for at least six consecutive months immediately preceding the filing of the current pending plea for support. If the child is less than 6 months old, it is the state where the child lived from birth.
Controlling Order	Refers to the only order entitled to be enforced.
Initiating State	Refers to the state that sent a case to another state for it to be enforced.
Responding or Enforcing State	Refers to the state that received a case from another state for the purpose of having it enforced.
Jurisdiction	Refers to the authority which a court (State) has over a person(s), case(s), or geographic location(s).
Continuous Exclusive Jurisdiction (CEJ)	Continuous Exclusive Jurisdiction is based on whether or not the parties (NCP, CP and or Child) continue to live in that state.

A state can lose CEJ if:

1. None of the parties live in that state.

OR

2. Each individual party to whom the support order pertains files written consent notifying the CEJ state that the party wishes to have the child support enforcement agency or court in another state modify the order, which would then give the new state CEJ. However, even if a state does lose its CEJ, its order remains valid and may be registered in another state for enforcement. Under UIFSA, the state that issued (filed) a support order has CEJ as long as that state remains the residential state of the non-custodial parent, custodial parent, or child for whom that support order pertains.

SO, WHO CONTROLS AN ORDER WHEN . . .

. . . one child support order exists?
In this case, the child support agency or court that issued (filed) the order controls it and has CEJ.

. . . two or more child support orders exist, but only one has CEJ?
In this case, the child support agency or court that has CEJ controls the order.

. . . more than one child support agency or court CAN claim CEJ?
In this case, the order filed by the child's current home state is the controlling order.

. . . more than one child support agency or court *can* claim CEJ, *but* the child's home state does not have an order?
In this case, the most recent order of those that do exist is the controlling order and has CEJ.

. . . there are multiple orders and none of the child support agencies or courts has CEJ?
In this case, any of the states involved could file a new order. Upon the filing thereof, the new order will become the controlling order, thereby assuming CEJ. With regard to methods of enforcement for UIFSA orders, it is the law of the enforcing state that will be used, not the enforcement methods of the initiating state, even though it has CEJ.

UIFSA & URESA Comparison

There are various differences in the UIFSA & URESA. The following are a few of them:

TERMINOLOGY	
Tribunal	
UIFSA	**URESA**
Tribunal includes courts as well as administrative agencies which establish, enforce, and modify support orders.	This is a judicial remedy, so only the courts can administer its provisions. The term "tribunal" is not used in URESA.

Definition of Support	
UIFSA	**URESA**
Defines support as inclusion of health care, interest and attorney fees.	Does not make known the definition of support.
Continuing Exclusive Jurisdiction (CEJ)	
UIFSA	**URESA**
Provides for only one support order at one time and declares that order to be the controlling order.	Has no rule for this. That is why there could be multiple orders at the same time.
Initiation of a Case	
UIFSA	**URESA**
Does not require a formal hearing and it is not necessary for the initiating jurisdiction to ask a judge to sign a certificate and order to send to the responding jurisdiction. It is possible for a party in the initiating state to file an action directly in the responding state without going through the initiating state.	Requires the initiating court's review and signature of a "certificate" specifying that the initiating jurisdiction finds the pleadings reflect a basis upon which the responding state may determine a duty of support.
Availability of Remedies	
UIFSA	**URESA**
Remedies for an order are available to the non-custodial and the custodial parents.	Remedies for an order are available to the custodial parent ONLY.

Safeguarding Information	
UIFSA	**URESA**
Authorizes nondisclosure of identifying information when the health, safety, or liberty of a party or child is at risk.	Does not have a similar provision.

Visitation	
UIFSA	**URESA**
Clarifies visitation as being separate from the issue of support. Visitation issues cannot be used as defense of nonsupport.	Has a similar provision.

Petitioners Responsibility of Cost & Fees	
UIFSA	**URESA**
Non-custodial parent and custodial parent can file a case without payment of cost and fees.	Free filing for custodial parent only; non-custodial parent must pay.

ESTABLISHMENT ISSUES	
Paternity	
UIFSA	**URESA**
Clearly authorizes the establishment of parentage in an interstate proceeding, even if it is not coupled with a proceeding to establish support. It also provides for setting temporary support based on a paternity acknowledgement.	Authorizes paternity establishment but is unclear as to whether action must be coupled with a support proceeding. In some states, support establishment must be requested as well. This is a two-state process with no explicit provisions.

Temporary Support	
UIFSA	**URESA**
Provides for a temporary support order based on a paternity acknowledgement or other clear and convincing evidence (genetic tests) that the defendant is the child's parent.	Does not have a specific provision for temporary orders.
Long-Arm Jurisdiction	
UIFSA	**URESA**
Provides for the assertion of long-arm jurisdiction over a nonresident up to the limits of the U.S. Supreme Court's decision in Kulko v. Superior Court of California, 436 U.S. 84 (1978) (i.e., the residence of a child in a state does not, by itself, give that state personal jurisdiction over the child's nonresident parent). UIFSA's long-arm provisions are based upon the NCP's conduct with the state.	Does not have a similar provision.

ENFORCEMENT ISSUES	
UIFSA	**URESA**
UIFSA has 3 enforcement mechanisms. 1) Direct Enforcement, which allows a state to initiate local enforcement remedies on a nonresident if personal jurisdiction over the nonresident can be obtained by UIFSA's long-arm provisions. If personal jurisdiction over the NCP is not present, an income withholding order may be mailed directly to the individual's employer in another state (if that state adopted UIFSA's direct income withholding provision). 2) Administrative Enforcement without registration: This allows the responding state, with administrative enforcement procedures, to initiate administrative enforcement procedures without Registering the order. 3) Registration for Enforcement: This is the UIFSA enforcement mechanism that provides access to the full range of enforcement remedies.	Does not have a similar provision for direct wage withholding. Enforcement is a two-state process by establishing a new order or against a registration.

MODIFICATION ISSUES	
Continuing Exclusive Jurisdiction (CEJ)	
UIFSA	**URESA**
Has a process to determine which state can modify an order.	Has nothing to determine who can or cannot modify an order.
Spousal Support Modification	
UIFSA	**URESA**
Spousal support can only be modified by the original state that issued it.	Treats child support and spousal support the same.

CHOICE OF LAW ISSUES	
Enforcement of Support Order	
UIFSA	**URESA**
Provides that the procedures and laws of the responding state apply in enforcement issues. There are two exceptions: 1) The law of the issuing state governs the interpretation of the order being enforced. 2) If the issuing and responding states have different statutes of limitations for enforcement, the longest statute of limitations applies.	Applies the law of the state where the NCP was present for the period during which support is sought. Otherwise, the law of the responding state is used.
Determination of Support Amount	
UIFSA and URESA both apply guidelines of the responding State.	

EVIDENTIARY PROVISIONS	
Electronic Information Transfer	
UIFSA	**URESA**
Authorizes electronic information transfer, testimony or deposition by telephone conference, and interstate discovery.	Does not have a similar provision.
Records	
UIFSA	**URESA**
Allows copies of payment records from another State, copies of health care bills, and facsimile copies as admissible evidence.	Does not have a similar provision.

COMMUNICATION BETWEEN TRIBUNALS	
UIFSA	**URESA**
States that tribunals of different states may communicate with each other to obtain information about the laws of the other state or orders of the other tribunal.	Does not have a similar provision.

If you are interested in knowing more about this subject contact the Office of Child Support Enforcement Public Information and Inquiries Office.

REFERENCED IN THIS CHAPTER

[1] OCSE UIFSA Handbook

CHAPTER 7

Wage Garnishments & Arrears

Wage Garnishment

Order to Withhold Income, Administrative Writ of Withholdings, Writ of Garnishment, Payroll Deduction Notice, etc; no matter what they are called, they all involve deductions made from an individual's earnings. According to labor law, wage garnishments do not include voluntary wage assignments made by an employee to an employer[1].

Earnings are any wages, salary, commission, bonuses, or other income[2]. Earnings also include payments from pension or retirement programs as well. Tips are generally not considered earnings for the purposes of the wage garnishment law, which "applies to all 50 states, the District of Columbia and all U.S. territories and possessions[3]."

The portions of earnings that are subject to garnishment are called "disposable earnings." *Disposable earnings* are the employee's earnings remaining after legally required deductions are withheld for Federal income tax, social security taxes, state and city tax, unemployment insurance and deductions required under state employee's retirement systems[4]. Other deductions which are not required by law (e.g. union dues, health and life insurance, charitable contributions, etc.) are not subtracted from gross earnings when calculating the amount of disposable earnings for garnishment purposes. However, a state may choose to make deductions for these items when calculating a support obligation.

Garnishment Limitations

CCPA (Consumer Credit Protection Act) limits the amount of individuals' disposable earnings which may be garnished for any work week to a maximum of *25%* or 30 times the minimum wage (whichever is less) for commercial (ordinary) garnishments[5]. As for support garnishments, the maximum limitations of individuals' disposable earnings are as follows:

- *50%—if the individual has a second family to support* <u>and</u>
- a *maximum of 60%-if the individual has no second family to support.*
- If an individual is in arrears on their obligation of support, *maximums are increased by 5% (55% & 65%)*, provided that the payments for arrears are at least 12 weeks overdue.

These percentage restrictions (limitations) do not apply to debts due for any state or federal taxes or Chapter 13 Bankruptcy debt(s)[6]. In fact, there are no restrictions on the amount that may be withheld in these particular instances[7].

Garnishment Priority & Restrictions on Garnishments

When the disposable earnings of an individual are subject to more than one garnishment, it generally raises the following questions: Can an individual's disposable earnings be subject to more than one garnishment at the same time? If so, how is it determined?

Priority of garnishments are determined by state law, or federal law, but not by the CCPA[8]. Therefore, you may find that this practice varies from one state to another. Because there are no limits as to how much may be garnished for tax or Chapter 13 Bankruptcy debt, there may be cases where an individual will have more than one garnishment in effect at the same time.

Even in these cases the maximum garnishment of an individual's disposable earnings cannot exceed the limits of the CCPA: 25% for commercial (ordinary) garnishments, and 50%-65% (whichever is applicable) for support garnishments[9]."

The following examples are based on the first garnishment entered as if it has garnishment priority in accordance with state law. They are similar to those outlined at 29 CFR 870.11 (b)(2)(i),(ii),(iii),(iv) (2010).

[10]**Example 1:** 30 % of an individual's disposable earnings are currently being garnished for a tax debt. Afterwards

a garnishment for support is entered. While the garnishment for support is allowed, it cannot exceed 20%-35% (difference between the 30% currently being garnished for tax debt and the 50%-65% applicable maximum allowed for support garnishments).

[11]**Example 2:** 30% of an individual's disposable earnings are currently being garnished for support. Afterwards, a garnishment for an ordinary debt is sought. The ordinary debt garnishment is not permitted because the maximum garnishment amount of 25% has been exceeded.

[12]**Example 3:** 65% of an individual's disposable earnings are currently being garnished for tax and/or Chapter 13-Bankruptcy debt. Afterwards, a garnishment for support is sought. The support garnishment is not permitted because the maximum garnishment amount for support (up to 65%) has already been exceeded.

The CCPA restrictions do not prevent a state from having lower limits on garnishments[13]. Rather, it prevents states from setting higher limits than those set by the CCPA. Therefore, you may find that some states use a different percentage for garnishment limitations than that of the CCPA. For example, Washington State generally caps at 45% of an individual's net income for support garnishments[14]. In cases where state limitations are lower, the lower limitation applies.

If you have a question regarding *your* wage garnishment contact U.S. Dept. of Labor Wage & Hour Division's

Referral Line for the local office in your area 1-866-4USWAGE (1-866-487-9243).

Arrears

Assigned and unassigned child support arrears may be negotiated for reduction, purged after a lump sum payment has been made by the NCP, and/or suspended in some cases. In non-welfare cases, lowering or any other negotiation of this debt is at the discretion of the CP[15]. However, in cases where the CP is receiving child support services, the agency or court may review this agreement to ensure that the best interest of the child has been considered. In welfare assistance cases, any negotiation for purging of this debt by a lump sum payment is left at the discretion of the state to which the debt is owed.

Generally, when a current order for support expires due to emancipation of a child, and arrears still exist, current support continues at the same rate until all arrears are satisfied. This, like many other procedures, will depend on individual state practices.

There are cases with no current order for support, but where arrears do exist. States vary in their practice to satisfy arrears in these instances. For example, Connecticut has Arrearage Guidelines, which provide that in cases where there is an arrearage, and no current support order exists, a current support obligation is imputed for the child for whom the arrearage is owed. "The arrearage payment is established at: 20% of an imputed obligation—if the child is an un-emancipated minor, or 50% of an imputed obligation-if the child for whom the arrearage is owed is deceased, emancipated, or over the age of eighteen[16]." For more information on this topic, contact your state's child support enforcement administration.

Payments Toward Arrears by Wage Garnishment

You may have owed arrears at the time your order was established, or you may have accumulated them afterwards. In either case, your wage garnishment for current support will likely include payment toward those arrears. As well, there are a myriad of other methods used by child support enforcement administration to collect outstanding arrears, including tax refund interceptions and more outlined in the next chapter.

You will want to avoid overpayment on these arrears by monitoring your deductions. You should do this monthly, semi-annually, or annually depending on the amount of arrears you owe. For example, if you owe two or three hundred dollars in arrears, check payments made toward those arrears monthly. On the other hand, if you owe a few thousand dollars, annual check-ups will do. That way, when the arrears are paid in full you can request a modification to have your garnishment reduced by the amount of the payment toward arrears (if applicable). Arrears can accumulate quickly, and the same holds true of their reduction when payments are made regularly.

When it comes to garnishments, I have known few employers or payroll clerks to give detailed attention to anything more than the amount of a child support garnishment in full. An overpayment can easily occur when the payment toward arrears portion of your garnishment continues after the arrears are satisfied. Since states are allowed to charge interest and/or late payment fees on child support debts, you may want to contact your local agency to find out what amount of interest, if any, is being charged to your account. For more on the interest charged by states, see "ROUTINE FEES" in FYIs for NCPs section in the back of the book.

Limitations on Debt Recovery

Recovering payment and/or arrears accumulated when there has been a lapse of time in enforcing or establishing an order may not be possible if action is not taken within the time allowed under a state's statute of limitations. This issue was a contributing factor in matters relating to case summary #8.

These limitations do vary from one state to another. In cases regarding UIFSA orders, when states are working together to enforce an order, whichever state's law provides the longer limitations is the one that applies to that case[17].

Support Arrears and Bankruptcy

Many NCPs will attempt to seek relief from huge child support arrearage debt by filing for bankruptcy. However, child support debts, like alimony and family support debts, are non-dischargeable in bankruptcy. This means they will not disappear after your bankruptcy case is complete through discharge. If arrears are a problem and you have additional financial challenges (credit card debt, repossessions, medical bills, etc.), filing a bankruptcy may not be such a bad idea. Just because you cannot eliminate the child support debt does not mean you cannot find some form of relief through a bankruptcy if the remaining debt you have is adding difficulty to your financial situation. If this is a concern or you have questions contact a bankruptcy attorney.

Credit Bureau Report of Child Support Arrears

The name of the NCP and amount of overdue support owed may be reported to the consumer credit reporting agency. Wage garnishments may also be reported in some states. In community property states, child support debt may be reported for both the NCP and his/her current spouse. However, prior to dispensing this information to the credit bureau, the child support enforcement "agency must give *'advance notice'* to the NCP of the proposed release of information to the consumer credit reporting agency[18]." This notice should inform the NCP of the methods available for contesting the accuracy of the information and provide a reasonable time frame in which to contest the matter.

If you have been reported to the credit agency and the information is incorrect, you need to contact the child support enforcement agency that submitted this debt to review your case. If it turns out that the agency's information is incorrect, and the necessary steps are not made to correct the mistake, you should file an appropriate complaint with the credit bureau to which this debt was reported. If unsuccessful with either of these suggestions, contact the FTC (Federal Trade Commission) 1-877-FTC-HELP (382-4357).

REFERENCED IN THIS CHAPTER

1,2,3,4   *US DOL Employment Standards Administration Wage and Hour Division Fact Sheet #30: The Federal Wage Garnishment Law, Consumer Credit Protection Act Title 3 (CCPA), 2006.and 15 USC 1672(a)*

5   15 USC 1673(a),(1),(2)

6 & 7   29CFR870.11(a)(1)(i)(ii)(2) and *U.S. D.O.L. Employment Standards Administration Wage and Hour Division Fact Sheet #30: The Federal Wage Garnishment Law, Consumer Credit Protection Act Title 3 (CCPA), 2006. and 15 USC 1673(b) (2),(c),(b)(2)(A),(B),(C)*

8 & 9   29CFR870.11(b)(2)(1)(A)(B)

10, 11 & 12   29CFR870.11(b)(2)(i),(ii),(iii) (2006)

13   15 USC 1673(c)

14   Washington State Child Support Schedule—RCW26.19.065 (1998)

15   http://www.acf.hhs.gov/programs/cse/po1/PIQ/piq-00-03.htm

16   State of Connecticut Child Support and Arrearage Guidelines. CGS Section 46b-215a-4a. (d)(1),(2) (2009)

17   OCSE UIFSA Handbook

18   42USC666(a)(7)(B),(i)(ii) (2009)

CHAPTER 8

Tax Refund Issues

Certifications & Interceptions . . .

If you have ever had arrears you know all about these. Each year certification notices are sent to NCPs who are in arrears on their support obligation. Among other things, these state the time frame you are given to contest the amount of arrears you owe. Whatever the time frame is in your state, it is in your best interest to take advantage of the time stated in the notice.

Why is that so important? Your account has to be reviewed before any necessary adjustments can be made, and this is not a quick process. Unfortunately, many NCPs are so taken aback by the amount stated in these notices that they do not take the time to read the fine print. As a result, many certifications go unchallenged, and tax refund interceptions occur that may be improper.

Case Summary #7

Occupation: Salesman

Problem: Multiple tax refund interceptions and closing out of state case with arrears.

Alleged Arrears: $2,882.76

Mr. Dudley signed a Consent Agreement with an out-of-state child support enforcement agency. We will call this agency no.1. The agreement stated that he would pay $150 per month for current support, and an additional amount of $23 per month to satisfy arrears totaling $546.25. The arrears were due to the state for reimbursement of welfare benefits the CP and child received. Mr. Dudley's total obligation of $173 per month was made by wage garnishment.

A year later, there was a crisis in his family that required Mr. Dudley to relocate to his home state. Upon his return, he was unable to secure employment right away, so his child support fell about four months behind. That's where his problems began.

The following year, around February, Mr. Dudley received a letter from agency no.1 indicating that he owed $1,719.43 in child support arrears. He knew that there were lapses in payments due to his change in employment a year earlier, so he did not bother to question whether or not the amount of arrears indicated was accurate.

The following month, Mr. Dudley received a notice from the IRS stating that $450.00 had been intercepted by a local child support enforcement agency in the state where he lived for a past-due support obligation. We will call this agency no. 2. Assuming that agency no. 2 was acting on behalf of agency no.1's interstate child support order, he chose not to question this action either. He was expecting a tax refund check soon (estimated at $1,391) and was just happy they weren't taking it all.

Unfortunately, in the same week, he received two more interception notices; one was for $560, the other $381. Both interceptions were made by out of state agency no. 1. Just when Mr. Dudley thought it couldn't get any worse, he received another letter. This time, it was from agency no. 2. The letter stated that his child support was overdue by another $617.08.

Mr. Dudley was frustrated and contacted his caseworker at agency no.2 for help. She promised to do what she could to resolve the matter. However, she reminded him that the arrears to agency no.1 would still have to be paid. For months Mr. Dudley and his caseworker tried to settle the matter, but nothing was resolved. Agency no.1 informed Mr. Dudley that the case would not be closed, and that even if it could be closed, the arrears would have to be paid in full.

In January of the following year Mr. Dudley received a letter from agency no.1. It wasn't another notice, but was quite unusual. It was a letter inquiring of the whereabouts of the mother of Mr. Dudley's child. It stated that they were holding money that was due her, but did not know where she was. At that point, Mr. Dudley sought help outside of the child support enforcement agency. He called his attorney who then contacted me to consult and investigate the case.

Findings:

Mr. Dudley was aware that the CP and his child had recently relocated to the state where he lived. However, he was not aware that she had sought public assistance and thereby assigned support rights to both agency no.1 (out-of-state) and agency no.2 (local). Not only was agency no.2 collecting on the URESA Order for agency no.1, but it was doing so for itself also. A detailed findings report was prepared, and copies were sent to both agencies along with the current address of the CP.

Results:

Agency no. 1 corrected their information, properly credited all payments, and Mr. Dudley's case was closed without further incident. Mr. Dudley was issued a reimbursement check for overpayment of obligation in the amount of $2,385.00. This check was forwarded to Mr. Dudley's local child support enforcement agency—agency no. 2—and they adjusted their records. After deducting what Mr. Dudley really owed in arrears he received an unexpected reimbursement check in the amount of $1,969 for overpayment of obligation. Mr. Dudley's accurate amount of arrears was only $453, *not* $2,882.76 as stated by the child support enforcement agencies. The reimbursed amount did not include funds previously mentioned that were held for the CP as they were disbursed to her directly. BELIEVE IT OR NOT!

Child Support Debt, the Non-obligated Spouse and the Tax Refund!

Improper tax refund interceptions are a big problem for many that file joint tax returns. In fact, there are many of you reading this information at this very moment that will be expecting a tax refund for this tax year. Unfortunately, you may never see it if you or your spouse is said to have child support arrears.

Tax refunds intercepted from taxpayers that file a joint return are usually held for about "six months" pending the non-obligated spouse's filing to recoup their portion of the tax refund[1]. Most non-obligated spouses do not know that they can file the proper forms with the IRS to recoup their portion.

If you filed a joint tax return within the past six years and you were expecting a tax refund that was intercepted for child support debt, you may be able to get the non-obligated spouse's portion of those refunds back by filing an Injured Spouse Allocation Form 8379 with the IRS.

Case Summary #8

Occupation: Automotive Repairman

Problem: Seeking reduction in current support and payment arrangements to satisfy arrears without having his home levied and being subjected to other methods of enforcement.

Alleged Arrears: over $56,000

Mr. Cunningham was in the military when he married, had children with and then divorced his ex-wife. Mr.

Cunningham's ex-wife and children moved to another state following the divorce, but then moved from their original address in that state and he was never informed of their new address. Confident that his ex-wife knew where to find him, Mr. Cunningham believed that after he left the military and his allotment ceased, his ex-wife would contact him. He was wrong. So, life did what life does—it went on, as did Mr. Cunningham. Eventually he remarried and settled down.

More than ten years after his divorce became final, Mr. Cunningham received something in the mail. It was a Child Support Enforcement Consumer Credit Report Notification from an out-of-state child support enforcement agency. The notice informed him that he had a court-ordered judgment for child support of $400 per month, and that as of the date of the notice he owed an estimated $53,000 in overdue support. The notice further stated that he had 30 days from the date of receipt of this notice to contest the amounts before the information would be provided to the credit bureau for both Mr. Cunningham and his current spouse. He was also informed that the necessary steps were being taken to put a lien against his home in order to prevent him from using his property for any type of financial gain.

Mr. Cunningham had no desire to avoid paying support for his children. Had he known their whereabouts he would have been paying support all along. In fact, the first thing he wanted to know was how his children were doing. The most immediate problem for Mr. Cunningham was how he was going to get the money that was now being demanded of him. Distressed, Mr. Cunningham sought the services of an attorney who then consulted with me to troubleshoot. He needed help so I took the case.

Findings:
We had an account number and a docket number. We knew the court where the order was filed, and the date that the order was filed. There was only one thing missing—a copy of the support order itself. I contacted the clerk of the court. Unable to locate the actual order, I went back to the child support division to see if they had a copy of it. That's when things got interesting. Further investigation revealed *that no order had ever existed.*

Apparently Mr. Cunningham's ex-wife had assigned support rights to the state several years earlier when she first relocated and applied for welfare. At that time Mr. Cunningham was on active military duty. Therefore allotments from his military pay began going to the state as reimbursement for benefits. When the $400 per month allotments stopped the computer continued to input the $400 allotment amount as current support due each month thereafter, for over 10 years. Eventually, it reached the amount of arrears charged to Mr. Cunningham of *now,* more than $56,000 which included interest.

My investigation further revealed that while federal law provides (and this state's Consumer Credit Report Notification states) that Mr. Cunningham has 30 days in which to contest the amounts in the notice, the child support enforcement agency had already provided this negative information to the credit bureau for both Mr. Cunningham and his current spouse *before they were ever notified that the debt existed.*

Results:

This case turned out to be what is commonly referred to as an "unrighteous case". Since no child support order existed, the arrears and current amount of support being charged to Mr. Cunningham were found to be improper. Further, one of the two children involved was currently self-supporting and in the military, and the other child was said to be in the midst of being adopted by a step parent.

I worked with the agency to get Mr. Cunningham and his current spouse removed from the credit bureau reporting agency's file for the child support debt, and he was released from any further enforcement actions as well. Total arrears due in this case, $0! BELIEVE IT OR NOT!

Community Property States . . .

In my experience with improper tax refund interception cases, if the non-obligated spouse met the criteria for injured spouse, their portion of the joint refund was usually refunded to them. However, this was not the case for two individuals who lived in community property states. I will use a Louisiana case as an example. As a community property state, the child support obligation was considered a community debt. Therefore, the entire refund was kept. I found out later that, had the couple had an existing "separate property agreement," the non-obligated spouse would have received the appropriate portion of the joint refund. There are nine community property states in the U.S. Whether this is the procedure used for each of them I do not know. If you have questions or concerns I suggest that you contact the IRS @ 1-800-829-1040. They should be able to answer any of your questions definitively or visit www. irs.gov to download forms and instructions.

While you may be reimbursed for an improper tax refund interception, you may not be able to avoid an actual interception even when you do address it in a timely manner. This may have something to do with the fact that the tax refund offset information is sent to the tax divisions months before you receive the notice of certification for interception. Generally speaking, once certified there is only one way to be decertified. The agency who reported the debt must inform the tax divisions that the certified individual should be removed from the certification list. This is a procedure that is generally done only once a year, and not on an individual basis. However, "upon proof that a tax refund was improperly intercepted in whole, or in part, states are required to have procedures in place to reimburse the individual.²"

Here is some news you could use. If you are an NCP you may want to contact the IRS to see if you qualify to claim your child as a dependent even if you do not have custody. The IRS determines just who can claim an exemption for a dependent and under what circumstances. You might be surprised at what you find out.

For details contact the IRS to obtain a complete copy of Publication #501 or visit www.irs.gov to download a copy.

REFERENCED IN THIS CHAPTER

[1] US DHHS ACF PIQ-03-07—Hold Period for Joint, Non-IV-A Tax Refund Offsets

[2] 45CFR303.104(c)(2)

FYIs for NCPs

This section will provide an overview of four topics that are not mentioned anywhere else in the book. This information is generalized; to obtain specific information on an individual state's practice, contact the child support enforcement administration for that state. Log onto the following web page to access the state contact information where your child support enforcement agency is located: http://www.acf.hhs.gov/programs/css/resource/state-and-tribal-child-support-agency-contacts. Some of the information provided in this chapter was obtained from literature and publications received from the National Resource Center.

Assignment of Support Rights

Assigned support obligation means any support obligation that has been assigned to the state as a condition of receiving state welfare assistance, including any medical support obligation or payment for medical care from any third party[1]. The general term "child support" includes spousal support if they are both included in the same support order. If the whereabouts of the NCP or putative father are unknown, the recipients must also cooperate with the state in actions to: establish an order for child support; establish paternity (if necessary); and obtain medical support (if applicable). Cooperation is a requirement for applicants seeking cash and/or medical assistance from the state unless cooperation has been waived by the state for good cause. These assignments create a debt due to the state by the NCP, whether he or she has been previously made aware of it or not.

Routine and Other Fees Charged to NCPs

In addition to monthly obligations of support (including arrears) NCPs in many states are obligated to pay other fees, interest, etc. In some states "[NCPs] are charged ongoing case processing fees.[2]" Other fees may include, but are not limited to the following:

Tax Refund Offset Fee:

To cover cost of offset procedures, the IRS and State Income Tax Divisions are allowed to deduct a set payment amount from each tax refund intercepted[3]. While this fee is deducted directly from the NCP's tax refund, the full amount intercepted is said to be credited to the NCP's payment record.

In non-welfare cases when the CP is receiving child support services, the CP pays for any offset procedures.

These fees may vary among states; however, the cost is generally between \$16 and \$25 per interception. Some states have procedures where this fee may be recouped from the NCP.

Late Payment Fees:

States may impose late payment fees on NCPs who owe overdue support. However, the late fees should be applied according to federal standards of 3% to 6% of the overdue support amount. As to collection of late payment fees, they can only be collected after the full amount of overdue support is paid and all requirements for notice to the NCP have been met under state law. These fees cannot reduce the amount of current or overdue support that is paid to the individual to whom it is owed[4].

Employer Administrative Fees:

These are fees deducted from the NCP's wages to cover their employer's cost for processing a wage garnishment for child support[5]. These fees typically run around \$2.50 per deduction and are optional not mandatory. They can be assessed monthly, per remittance or in another way; it just depends on the state. In Georgia, fees are \$25 for first deduction and \$3 per remittance thereafter. Again, these fees are at the discretion of the employer. It should also be noted that these deductions are kept by the employer, not forwarded to the child support agency. The total amount an employer withholds for child support plus their employer administrative fee cannot exceed the maximum amount permitted under the CCPA of 50%-65% (whichever is applicable). Not all employers participate in this practice. If you have questions or concerns regarding this matter, contact the payroll office where you work.

> *You should know that when the amount of support and the employer administrative fee combined exceeds the maximum amount allowed to be withheld, the employer is instructed by the child support enforcement administration to take the entire amount of their employer administrative fee first, and then forward the child support payment of current support less the employer's administrative fee[6]. What does this process do to the NCP's child support payment for current support? Create arrears, or add to an existing debt!*

Child Support Agency Administrative Fees:

Most child support agencies charge monthly administrative fees to NCP's and CP's accounts to process their support payments. These costs range from state to state and are typically under $3.00 per month.

Paternity Testing Fees:

If genetic tests are ordered by the state child support enforcement agency, the agency pays the costs for these tests[7]. However, should paternity be established, the father who denied paternity has to reimburse the state for these costs. If the results of the initial tests are disputed by the NCP or CP additional testing can be requested. In these instances, however, the individual that disputes the results has to pay the costs of any additional testing in advance.

Social Security and Child Support

Social Security Disability Insurance (SSDI) benefits received by a child can be counted as child support payments only if these payments are received on the NCP's accounts[8]. This *is not* the case, however, where a dependent child receives benefits as a result of their own individual disability. SSI (Supplemental Security Income) is a form of public welfare. As well, it may not be used to calculate support because those payments are not derived from the claimant's earnings, but are a form of public welfare. If this is a concern, you may want to look into this further. You can contact the Social Security Administration by calling @ 1-800-772-1213 or contact the child support enforcement administration to find out what your state's practice is on this subject.

REFERENCED IN THIS CHAPTER

[1] Glossary and 45CFR301.1 (2010)

[2] *June Gibbs Brown, US DHHS Office of Inspector General, State Policies Used to Establish Child Support Orders for Low Income Non-custodial Parents, OEI, July 2000.*

[3] 45CFR303.72(i)(1)(2010)

[4] 45CFR302.75(a),(b)(1),(2),(3),(4) (2010)

[5 & 6] The ABC's of Child Support Enforcement Employer Overview Packet—Income Withholding insert, FAQ Section and http:// www.faq.acf.hhs.gov/cgi-bin/ employers.cfg.htm

[7] 42USC666(a)(5)(B)(ii)(I),(II) (2010)

[8] 29CFR870.11 (b)(2)(1)(A)(B)

In closing, I would like to say that I do not think for a moment that the few case summaries shared in this book are isolated incidents at all. Unfortunately, these incidents happened to honest, hard-working people, not "deadbeats." For this reason, I cannot stress to you enough the importance of monitoring your child support case and keeping track of the payments you make to that case. This is the only way to protect yourself from a similar unfortunate situation.

In the future, if you don't know the answer to a question that concerns your case, do not be afraid to ask someone who is qualified to give you an answer. Find out what's going on in your case. Do you have arrears? To whom are they due? How were they accumulated? Are the arrears for a reimbursement to the state? How long did the CP receive state benefits? Know what's going on with your child support case!

Many of the following acronyms and words used in this glossary are from the U.S. Dept. of HHS ACF OCSE Glossary of Child Support Terms.

Acronyms

ACF	Administration for Children and Families
AFDC	Aid to Families with Dependent Children
CCA	Consumer Credit Agencies
CCPA	Consumer Credit Protection Act
CEJ	Continuing Exclusive Jurisdiction to modify a support order
CP	Custodial Party
CSE	Child Support Enforcement Agency
CSPIA	Child Support Performance and Incentive Act of 1998
DHHS	United States Department of Health and Human Services
DCIA	Debt Collection Improvement Act
DOB	Date of Birth
EDI	Electronic Data Interchange
EFT	Electronic Funds Transfer
EVS	Enumeration and Verification System
FCR	Federal Case Registry of Child Support Orders
FFCCSOA	Full Faith and Credit for Child Support Orders Act
FPLS	Federal Parent Locator Service
FSA	Family Support Act

IRS	Internal Revenue Service
IV-A	Title IV-A of the Social Security Act
IV-D	Title IV-D of the Social Security Act
IV-E	Title IV-E of the Social Security Act
MAO	Medical Assistance Only
MSFIDM	Multistate Financial Institution Data Match
MSO	Monthly Support Obligation
NCP	Non-Custodial Parent
NDNH	National Directory of New Hires
NH	New Hire
OCSE	Federal Office of Child Support Enforcement
PF	Putative Father
PIQ	Policy Interpretation Question
PRWORA	Personal Responsibility and Work Opportunity Reconciliation Act of 1996
RURESA	Revised Uniform Reciprocal Enforcement of Support Act
SDNH	State Directory of New Hires
SDU	State Disbursement Unit
SESA	State Employment Security Agency
SPLS	State Parent Locator Service
SSA	Social Security Administration
SSN	Social Security Number
TANF	Temporary Assistance for Needy Families
UI	Unemployment Insurance
UIFSA	Uniform Interstate Family Support Act
UPA	Unreimbursed Public Assistance
URESA	Uniform Reciprocal Enforcement of Support Act

Glossary

Adjudication—The entry of a judgment, decree, or order by a judge or other decision-maker such as a master, referee, or hearing officer based on the evidence submitted by the parties.

Administrative Procedure—Method by which support orders are made and enforced by an executive agency rather than by courts and judges.

Administration for Children and Families (ACF)—The agency in the Department of Health and Human Services (DHHS) that houses the Office of Child Support Enforcement (OCSE).

Aid to Families with Dependent Children (AFDC)—Former entitlement program that made public assistance payments on behalf of children who did not have the financial support of one of their parents by reason of death, disability, or continued absence from the home; known in many States as ADC (Aid to Dependent Children). This term was replaced with Temporary Aid to Needy Families (TANF) under the Personal Responsibility and Work Opportunity Reconciliation Act (PRWORA).

Arrearage—Past due, unpaid child support owed by the non-custodial parent. If the parent has arrearages, s/he is said to be "in arrears."

Assignment of Support Rights—The legal procedure by which a person receiving public assistance agrees to turn over to the State any right to child support, including arrearages, paid by the non-custodial parent in exchange for receipt of a cash assistance grant and other benefits. States can then use a portion of said child support to defray or recoup the public assistance expenditure.

Burden of Proof—The duty of a party to produce the greater weight of evidence on a point at issue.

Case—a collection of people associated with a particular child support order, court hearing, and/or request for IV-D services. This typically includes a Custodial Party (CP), a dependent(s), and a Non-custodial Parent (NCP) and/or Putative Father (PF).

Caseload—This defines a case as a parent (mother, father or putative/alleged father who is or eventually **might become** responsible under law for the support of a child.

Case ID—Unique identification number assigned to a case.

Child Support Enforcement (CSE) Agency—State agency that locates non-custodial parents (NCPs) or putative fathers (PF), establishes, enforces, and modifies child support, and collects and distributes child support money. This agency is operated by state or local government according to the Child Support Enforcement Program guidelines as set forth in Title IV-D of the Social Security Act, also known as "IV-D Agency". These agencies exist in every state.

Child Support Pass-Through—Provision by which at least $50 from a child support payment collected on behalf of a public assistance recipient is disbursed directly to the custodial parent. The Personal Responsibility and Work Opportunity Reconciliation Act (PRWORA) of 1996 eliminated the pass-through effective October 1, 1996. A few states have elected to retain the pass-through, paying it out of state, rather than Federal, money. Also known as Child Support "Disregard."

Client—A term often used to refer to the recipient of a TANF grant or IV-D services.

Common Law—A body of law developed from judicial decisions or custom rather than legislative enactments.

Complainant—Person who seeks to initiate court proceedings against another person. In a civil case the complainant is the plaintiff; in a criminal case the complainant is the state.

Complaint—The formal written document filed in a court whereby the complainant sets forth the names of the parties, the allegations, and the request for relief sought, sometimes called the initial pleading or petition.

Consent Agreement—Voluntary written admission of paternity or responsibility for child support.

Consumer Credit Agencies (CCA)—Private agencies that a state can use to locate obligors to establish and enforce child support.

Consumer Credit Protection Act (CCPA)—Federal law that limits the amount that may be withheld from earnings to satisfy child support obligations.

Cooperation—A condition of TANF eligibility whereby the recipient is required to cooperate with the child support agency in identifying and locating the non-custodial parent, establishing paternity, and/or obtaining child support payments.

Court Order—A legally-binding edict issued by a court of law. Issued by a magistrate, judge, or properly empowered administrative officer. A court order related to child support can dictate how often, how much, what kind of support a non-custodial parent is to pay, how long he or she is to pay it, and whether an employer must withhold support from his/her wages.

Custodial Party (CP)—The person who has primary care, custody, and control of the children.

Custody Order—Legally binding determination that establishes with whom a child shall live. The meaning of different types of custody terms (e.g., Joint Custody, Shared Custody, Split Custody) varies from state to state.

Decree—The judicial decision of a litigated action, usually in "equitable" cases such as divorce (as opposed to cases in law in which judgments are entered).

Default—The failure of a defendant to file an answer or appear in a civil case within the prescribed time after having been properly served with a summons and complaint.

Defendant—The person against whom a civil or criminal proceeding is begun.

Dependent—A child who is under the care of someone else. Most children who are eligible to receive child support must be a dependent. The child ceases to be a dependent when they reach the "age of emancipation" as determined by state law, but depending on the state's provisions, may remain eligible for child support for a period after they are emancipated.

Disbursement—The paying out of collected child support funds.

Disposition—The court's decision of what should be done about a dispute that has been brought to its attention. For instance, the disposition of the court may be that child support is ordered or an obligation is modified.

Distribution—The allocation of collected child support to the various types of debt within a child support case, as specified in 45 CFR 302.51 (e.g., monthly support obligations, arrears, ordered arrears, etc.).

Electronic Data Interchange (EDI)—Process by which information regarding an Electronic Funds Transfer (EFT) transaction is transmitted electronically along with the EFT funds transfer.

Escheat—when payment and/or property are reverted (go back to) the state when no legal heir(s) or owner(s) can be located.

Establishment—The process of proving paternity and/or obtaining a court or administrative order to put a child support obligation in place.

Extended Visitation—This typically refers to any visitation that goes beyond general visitation (i.e. 72-73 days per year).

Family Support Act—Law passed in 1988, with two major mandates: Immediate Wage Withholding, unless courts find that there is good cause not to require such withholding, or there is a written agreement between both parties requiring an alternative arrangement; and Guidelines for Child Support Award Amounts, which requires states to use guidelines to determine the amount of support for each family, unless they are rebutted by a written finding that applying the guidelines would be inappropriate to the case.

Federal Parent Locator Service (FPLS)—A computerized national location network operated by the Federal Office of Child Support (OCSE) of the Administration for Children and Families (ACF), within the Department of Health and Human Services (DHHS). FPLS obtains address and employer information, as well as data on child support cases in every state, compares them and returns matches to the appropriate states.

Full Faith and Credit—Doctrine under which a state must honor an order or judgment entered in another state.

Good Cause—A legal reason for which a Temporary Assistance to Needy Families (TANF) recipient is excused from cooperating with the child support enforcement process, such as past physical harm by the child's father. It also includes situations where rape or incest resulted in the conception of the child and situations where the mother is considering placing the child for adoption.

Guidelines—A standard method for setting child support obligations based on the income of the parent(s) and other factors determined by state law. The Family Support Act of 1988 requires states to use guidelines to determine the amount of support for each family, unless they are rebutted by a written finding that applying the guidelines would be inappropriate to the case.

IV-A (Public Assistance Programs)

IV-A Case—A child support case in which a custodial parent and children are receiving public assistance benefits under the State's IV-A program, which is funded under Title IV-A of the Social Security Act. Applicants for assistance from IV-A programs are automatically referred to their State IV-D agency in order to identify and locate the non-custodial parent, establish paternity and/or a child support order, and/or obtain child support payments. This allows the state to recoup or defray some of its public assistance expenditures with funds from the non-custodial parent.

IV-D (Child Support Services)

IV-D Case—A child support case where at least one of the parties, either the custodial party (CP) or the non—custodial parent (NCP), has requested or received IV-D services from the State's IV-D agency. A IV-D case is composed of a custodial party, non-custodial parent or putative father, and dependent(s).

IV-E (State Foster Care)

IV-E Case—A child support case in which the state is providing benefits or services under Title IV-E of the Social Security Act to a person, family, or institution that is raising a child (or children) that is not their own. As with other public assistance cases, recipients are referred to their state IV-D agency in order to identify and locate the non-custodial parent, establish paternity and/or a child support order, and/or obtain child support payments.

Imputed Income—Fringe benefits provided to employees that may be taxable but which cannot be counted as additional disposable income that is subject to child support obligations. It is also an estimated income amount derived by child support enforcement used to calculate a child support obligation.

Incentive Payments—Payments paid to states by federal government for collecting support payments, establishing paternity, establishing court orders, and meeting other performance standards.

Initiating Jurisdiction—The state or county court or administrative agency that sends a request for action to another jurisdiction in interstate child support cases. The requested action can include a request for wage withholding or for review and adjustment of existing child support obligations.

Intercept—A method of securing child support by taking a portion of non-wage payments made to a non-custodial parent. Non-wage payments subject to interception include federal tax refunds, state tax refunds, unemployment benefits, and disability benefits.

Interstate Cases—Cases in which the dependent child and non-custodial parent (NCP) live in different states, or where two or more states are involved in some case activity, such as enforcement.

Joint Custody—When parents share legal and/or physical custody of the children.

Judgment—The official decision or finding of a judge or administrative agency hearing officer upon the respective rights and claims of the parties to an action; also known as a decree or order and may include the "findings of fact and conclusions of law."

Judicial Remedies—A general designation for a court's enforcement of child support obligations.

Jurisdiction—The legal authority which a court or administrative agency has over particular persons and over certain types of cases, usually in a defined geographical area.

Legal Father—A man who is recognized by law as the male parent of a child.

Lien—A claim upon property to prevent sale or transfer of that property until a debt is satisfied.

Litigation—A civil action in which a controversy is brought before the court.

Locate—Process by which a non-custodial parent (NCP) or putative father (PF) is found for the purpose of establishing paternity, establishing and/or enforcing a child support obligation, establishing custody and visitation rights, processing adoption or foster care cases, and investigating parental kidnapping.

Motion—An application to the court requesting an order or rule in favor of the party that is filing the motion. Motions are generally made in reference to a pending action and may address a matter in the court's discretion or concern a point of law.

Multi-state Employer—An organization that hires and employs people in two or more states. The multi-state employer conducts business within each state and the employees are required to pay taxes in the state where they work. Single-state employers and multi-state employers are required by law to report all new hires to the State Directory of New Hires (SDNH) operated by their State government. However, unlike single-state employers, they have the option to report all of their new hires to the SDNH of only one state in which they do business rather than to all of them.

National Directory of New Hires (NDNH)—A national database containing New Hire (NH) and Quarterly Wage (QW) data from every state and federal agency and Unemployment Insurance (UI) data from State Employment Security Agencies (SESAs).

New Hire Reporting—Program that requires that all employers report newly hired employees to the State Directory of New Hires (SDNH) in their state. This data is then submitted to the National Directory of New Hires (NDNH), where it is compared against child support order information contained in the Federal Case Registry (FCR) for possible enforcement of child support obligations by wage garnishment. Some data is also made available for states to find new hires that have been receiving unemployment insurance or other public benefits for which they may no longer be eligible, helping States to reduce waste and fraud.

Non-custodial Parent (NCP)—This is the parent who does not have primary care, custody, or control of the child and has an obligation to pay child support, also referred to as the obligor.

Non-IV-A Case—This is a support case in which the custodial parent has requested IV-D services but is not receiving Temporary Assistance to Needy Families (TANF), also known as a non-TANF case.

Non-IV-D Orders—A child support order handled by a private attorney as opposed to the state/local child support enforcement (IV-D) agency.

Obligated—A term meaning that a non-custodial parent (NCP) is required to meet the financial terms of a court or administrative order.

Obligation—Amount of money to be paid as support by a non-custodial parent (NCP). This can take the form of financial support for the child, medical support, or spousal support. An obligation is a recurring, ongoing obligation, not a onetime debt such as an assessment.

Obligee—The person, state agency, or other institution to which a child support is owed (also referred to as custodial party when the money is owed to the person with primary custody of the child).

Obligor—The person who is obliged to pay child support (also referred to as the non-custodial parent or NCP).

Offset—Amount of money intercepted from a parent's state or federal income tax refund, or from an administrative payment such as federal retirement benefits, in order to satisfy a child support debt.

Order—Direction of a magistrate, judge, or properly empowered administrative officer. *(See also: Court Order and Support Order)*

Paternity—Legal determination of fatherhood. Paternity must be established before child or medical support can be ordered.

Payee—Person or organization in whose name child support money is paid.

Payor—Person who makes a payment; usually non-custodial parents or someone acting on their behalf, or a custodial party who is repaying a receivable.

Personal Responsibility and Work Opportunity Reconciliation Act of 1996 (PRWORA)—Legislation that provides a number of requirements for employers, public licensing agencies, financial institutions, as well as state and federal child support agencies, to assist in the location of non-custodial parents and the establishment, enforcement, and collection of child support. This legislation created the New Hire Reporting program and the state and federal Case Registries.

Physical Custody—Sharing a residence with a child.

Plaintiff—A person who brings an action; the party who complains or sues in a civil case.

Pleadings—Statements or allegations, presented in logical and legal form, which constitute a plaintiff's cause of action or a defendant's grounds of defense.

Policy Interpretation Question (PIQ)—An official reply by the Federal Office of Child Support Enforcement (OCSE) to an inquiry submitted by a state child support agency concerning application of policy. Although questions often arise from a specific practice or situation, the responses are official statements of OCSE policy on the issue.

Proceeding—The conduct of business before a judge or administrative hearing officer.

Private Case—Known as a non-IV-D case, it is a support case where the custodial parent to whom child support is owed is not receiving IV-A benefits or IV-D services.

Public Assistance—Benefits granted from State or Federal programs to aid eligible recipients (eligibility requirements vary between particular programs). Applicants for certain types of public assistance (e.g., Temporary Assistance to Needy Families or TANF) are automatically referred to their State IV-D agency identify and locate the non-custodial parent, establish paternity, and/or obtain child support payments. This allows the State to recoup or defray some of its public assistance expenditures with funds from the non-custodial parent.

Putative Father (PF)—The person alleged to be the father of the child but who has not yet been medically or legally declared to be the Legal Father.

Qualified Medical Child Support Order (QMCSO)—An order, decree, or judgment, including approval of a settlement agreement, issued by a court or administrative agency of competent jurisdiction that provides for medical support for a child of a participant under a group health plan or provides for health benefit coverage to such child.

Quasi-Judicial—A framework or procedure under the auspices of a state's judicial branch in which court officers other than judges process, establish, enforce and modify support orders, usually subject to judicial review. The court officer may be a magistrate, a clerk, master, or court examiner. He or she may or may not have to be an attorney, depending on the state's law.

Recipient—A person or organization that receives support funds and/or Temporary Assistance to Needy Families (TANF) payments.

Reciprocity—A relationship in which one state grants certain privileges to other states on the condition that they receive the same privilege.

Respondent—The party answering a petition or motion.

Responding Jurisdiction—The court or administrative agency with jurisdiction over a non-custodial parent or child support order on which an initiating state has requested action.

Review and Adjustment—Process in which current financial information is obtained from both parties in a child support case and evaluated to decide if a support order needs to be adjusted.

Service of Process—This is the delivery of a writ or summons to a party for the purpose of obtaining jurisdiction over that party.

Service by Publication—Service of process accomplished by publishing a notice in a newspaper or by posting on a bulletin board of a courthouse or other public facility, after a court determines that other means of service are impractical or have been unsuccessful. This procedure is not legal in every state.

Show Cause—A court order directing a person to appear and bring forth any evidence as to why the remedies stated in the order should not be confirmed or executed. A show cause order is usually based on a motion and affidavit asking for relief.

Sole Custody—When one parent has primary physical custody of the child.

Split Custody—When parents have more than one child and each parent has physical custody of one or more of the children.

Spousal Support—Court ordered support of a spouse or ex-spouse; also referred to as maintenance or alimony.

State Disbursement Unit (SDU)—The single site in each state where all child support payments are processed. Upon implementation of centralized collections, each state will designate its State Disbursement Unit, or SDU, to which all withheld child support payments should be sent.

Subpoena—A process issued by a court compelling a witness to appear at a judicial proceeding. Sometimes the process will also direct the witness to bring documentary evidence to the court.

Summons—A notice to a defendant that an action against him or her has been commenced in the court issuing the summons and that a judgment will be taken against him or her if the complaint is not answered within a certain time.

Temporary Assistance to Needy Families (TANF)—Time-limited public assistance payments made to poor families, based on Title IV-A of the Social Security Act. TANF replaced Aid to Families with Dependent Children (AFDC—otherwise known as welfare) when the Personal Responsibility and Work Opportunity Reconciliation Act (PRWORA) was signed into law in 1996.

Temporary Custody—When custody is temporarily awarded until the court makes a final decision for permanent custody.

Third Party Liability—A category under which the state pays the difference between the amount of the medical bill and the amount the insurance company has paid. This occurs only when a public assistance recipient has medical insurance in addition to coverage provided by the public assistance program.

Tribunal—The court, administrative agency, or quasi-judicial agency authorized to establish or modify support orders or to determine parentage.

Unreimbursed Public Assistance (UPA)—Money paid in the form of public assistance (for example, TANF or older AFDC expenditures) which has not yet been recovered from the non-custodial parent (NCP).

Notes